# THE PERFECTION OF NOTHING
## REFLECTIONS ON SPIRITUAL PRACTICE

**RICK LEWIS**

HOHM PRESS
Prescott, Arizona

Cover design: Kim Johansen
Layout and design: Advanced Media Concepts, Palm Springs, Calif. and Kubera Services, Prescott, Arizona

Library of Congress Cataloging in Publication Data:

Lewis, Rick, 1961-
    The perfection of nothing / Rick Lewis.
        p. cm.
    ISBN 1-890772-02-X (alk. paper)
    1. Spiritual life. I. Title.

BL624 .L5 2000
291.4'4--dc21

00-040-927


HOHM PRESS
P.O. Box 2501
Prescott, AZ 86302
800-381-2700
http://www.hohmpress.com

This book was printed in the U.S.A. on acid-free paper using soy ink.

# THE PERFECTION OF NOTHING
## REFLECTIONS ON SPIRITUAL PRACTICE

*For Beloved Saqi*

# Acknowledgments

These writings belong to the radical, radiant and Divine Influence of my Teacher, Mr. Khepa Lee Baul. It is to Him and All that He is that any merit is due. It is He who deserves any acknowledgment and to whom I am inexpressibly grateful.

My love and gratitude go to my first teacher, my father, who has demonstrated discipline, kindness, inner strength, a thirst for the truth, and equanimity in his actions and in his life. Here's to you, Dad. Thanks for giving me and many others the benefit of the doubt.

All my love to my wife Zoë and children, Nathaniel and Ruby, who have shown me the joy of human relationship.

A special thank you to Zoë for her love and companionship on the path.

My love and thanks to my mother, Nancy, whose deft skill as my editor shines in its invisibility, yet pales in comparison to the giant heart she has brought to her mothering.

My thanks and regard to the sangha body of the Hohm Community, especially to Red Hawk and Purna, who were instrumental in introducing me to Mr. Lee, and for the support they have generously given to me in this work.

Finally, my thanks to all the friends over the years who have encouraged me to write.

# Contents

# Prologue

*Akhanda-mandalaa-kaaram*
 *vyaaptam yena charaa-charam,*
*Tat-padam darshitam yena*
 *tasmai shree-gurave namah.*

Salutations to Sri Guru, who has revealed that state
which pervades the entire sphere of this universe, which
is comprised of animate and inanimate objects.

*Sarva-shruti-shiro-ratna-*
 *viraajita-padaam-bujah,*
*Vedaan-taambuja-sooryo yas-*
 *tasmai shree-gurave namah.*

Salutations to Sri Guru; his lotus feet are adorned with
the crest-jewels (the mahavakyas—the great
Upanishandic statements) of all Vedas. He is the sun to
the lotus of Vedanta (in the sense that his light causes
spiritual truths to bloom).

*Yasya smarana-maatrena*
 *jnaana-mutpadyate svayam,*
*Ya eva sarva-sampraaptis-*
 *tasmai shree-gurave namah.*

Salutations to Sri Guru, by merely remembering whom
knowledge arises spontaneously. He is all attainments.

*Chaitanyam shaashvatam shaantam*
 *vyomaa-teetam niranjanam,*
*Naada-bindu-kalaateetam*
 *tasmai shree-gurave namah.*

Salutations to Sri Guru; he is Consciousness, which is
eternal, peaceful, stainless and transcends the sky. He
is beyond nada (primordial sound), bindu (ultimate
point) and kala (manifestation of the world).

*Sthaavaram jangamam chaiva*
 *tathaa chaiva charaa-charam,*
*Vyaaptam yena jagat-sarvam*
 *tasmai shree-gurave namah.*

Salutations to Sri Guru, who pervades this entire
world, consisting of the movable and immovable, and
also the animate and inanimate.

*Jnaana-shakti-samaa-roodhas-*
*tattva-maalaa-vibhoo-shitah,*
*Bhukti-mukti-pradaataaya*
*tasmai shree-gurave namah.*

Salutations to Sri Guru; he is firmly established in the
power of knowledge and is adorned with the garland
of tattvas. He grants worldly fulfillment as well as salvation.

*Aneka-janma-sampraapta*
*sarva-karma-vidaahine,*
*Svaatma-jnaana-prabhaa-vena*
*tasmai shree-gurave namah.*

Salutations to Sri Guru, who by [imparting] the power
of Self-knowledge burns up all the karmas acquired
through countless lives.

*Na guro-radhikam tattvam*
*na guro-radhikam tapah,*
*Tattvam jnaanaat-param naasti*
*tasmai shree-gurave namah.*

Salutations to Sri Guru. There is no truth higher than
the Guru, no austerity greater than [service to] the Guru,
no truth greater than the knowledge [of him].

*Mannaathah shree-jagan-naatho*
*mad-guru-strijagad-guruh,*
*Mamaatmaa sarva-bhootaatmaa*
*tasmai shree-gurave namah.*

Salutations to Sri Guru. My Lord is the lord of the universe.
My Guru is the Guru of the three worlds. My Self is the Self
of all beings.

Verses 67 - 75, *The Guru Gita*

# Introduction

*My Father alone exists. There is nothing else, nobody else—past, present, future—here, there, everywhere! Anywhere. There's nothing else, nobody else. My Father alone! My Father alone! My Father alone. That is the only existence. Nothing else exists, nobody else exists. Nothing is separate, nothing isolated. All in Father, Father in all—near, nearest, far, far, farthest, Father alone! Past, past . . . very very far away in past, present, future, far, far away in future . . . there is only one existence . . . of my Father . . . indivisible, total, whole, absolute . . . There is nothing else, nobody else.*

YOGI RAMSURATKUMAR

*God's whole purpose for creating the earth is to have a good time over nothing.*

LEE LOZOWICK

There are only three words in the universe. The first of the three words that came to be represents the totality of existence: the All which encompasses the whole of Reality.

## God

Then came the second word. The word which preceded every form in existence. Before the embodiment of man, before time began, even before matter was a twinkle in God's eye, a word was unleashed from the nothingness of eternity which made all else imminent. The cork of the universe that, once loosed, allowed for a flood of possibilities that staggered even the Creator Himself. The creation of the second word gave birth to the totality of possibility.

## Is

Then there was a space of no-time in which the two words, "God is . . . ," produced the first question. "What?" This question was not posed in language, but appeared as the mood of inquiry, of Divine curiosity which, knowing no restraint, immediately happened upon the notion of relating to itself, playing with itself, confronting itself. This was the moment of "original desire," and from it gushed the third word—the first distinction in an otherwise undifferentiated creation—a word that took the Universe apart, scattered it into form, exploded it into functions and purpose; only because function, purpose, and form are required for relationship. Through this word, non-creation came to know itself as creation, and the totality of possibility became manifested over an infinite amount of space and time, gaining limitless perspectives for relationship to itself. The third word was . . .

## Everything

These three words together, "God Is Everything," describe the spontaneous and lawful condition of existence in its desire to know itself. It is the original immaculate conception in which nothingness has fashioned a second face from its own perfect emptiness, allowing for the contemplation and enjoyment of its own Heart. Each expression of second face is immaculately Divined, manifested for the pleasure of creation's own self-embrace, while universal consciousness rests in the constant remembrance that each expression is but its own. To sustain this play, each distinct facet of the second face itself was designed to forget; to play as if singular, individual, and separate. Except for one.

Into the midst of this design the universe gave one form that would play out its assigned separation, but have also the capacity for seeing back to its Creator, even while immersed in the grandest of creation's theater. This particular expression is called a human being.

A human being, in surrendering fully to the will of creation's pleasure, in submitting completely to the truest destiny of being human, embodies the possibility, and the only possibility in creation, for the perfection of Nothing.

# THE CONTEXT OF TRANSFORMATION

The daily world continually gestures to the Real world. The pettiness, the unimportance, the impermanence of the relative world is a springboard, an invitation to see past, beyond, and through to that Reality which radiates behind it, in complete support of it. A cloud that passes between one and the sun enhances appreciation for the sun itself. Though below it, the clouds should serve the sun this way.

The illusion is the advance man for the main act and sets the stage, prepares the audience for the Truth. The deeper the illusion and the more painful it all is, the more the Divine is exalted and vivified. This world is not a distraction at all. In the right context, this world is just the adornment of Truth—bringing attention to the Truth, like the gold bracelet around the ankle of the courtesan. Yes, the bracelet glitters, but look . . .

We must develop the ability to see through. It must cross our minds that there is a fundamentally and radically different way we could be using our attention; a way that serves evolution and Creation and all that we are in relationship to it.

ða.

The difference between doing psychological/translational work and spiritual/transformational work demands that we become educated about the appropriate focus of our attention. *Translational* work can be roughly described as messing with the potholes in our psychological driveway. The reason such work is translational and not *transformational** is this: The object of all inner growth and spiritual work is to reach Home, the true Self. The driveway, which represents the complete content of our psychological makeup, has only one rightful function. It is a buffer between the main road and Home. Most of the so-called spiritual work being taught and promoted nowadays falls into the trap of trying to shorten or eliminate the driveway—that is, the psychological realm. This is not only impossible, it is suicidal, and arises from the puritanical ignorance upon which a great deal of our culture is built and under the influence of which we suffer. The long and winding driveway protects the sanctuary of Home. The driveway is wanted, needed, and not a problem. A nice long driveway is preferable even. If our Home were overlooking the expressway, it would no longer be a Sanctuary. The driveway only becomes a problem when we cannot traverse its complete length in our vehicle and are therefore prevented from getting home. So if we succeed in getting rid of our driveway, we're really in trouble as far as our spirituality is concerned.

So at some point our culture looked at the puritans and the fanatics and realized they were only harming themselves, essentially working against what it means to be human. But people were still looking for something, so the "personal growth movement" got invented. The personal growth movement took a look at what went before and realized that it couldn't propose elimination of the driveway, so it opted for a slyer and sneakier form of driveway obsession called "the driveway improvement plan." In the personal growth modality the

---

* This distinction between translation and transformation was made elegantly and in-depth by Ken Wilber in "A Spirituality That Transforms," *What is Enlightenment?* Fall/Winter 1997, pp. 23-32.

entire focus of an individual's life is still psychological—that is, on the driveway—but the focus is on repair, renovation, and restoration techniques.

When there are so many potholes in our driveway that it is impossible to negotiate our vehicle along the length of it to our Home, then yes, we must attend to the repair of those potholes until we can navigate the driveway to the end. If, however, we have potholes in our driveway and it is still possible for our vehicle to get Home with a little attentive steering to avoid getting stuck in them but we choose instead to spend all our time fixing them up, perfecting them, smoothing them over, polishing them, fretting over their contents, their depth, how they got there, discussing strategies, methods, and therapies for repairing them, there are only two possible reasons for our behavior. One, we are actually terrified of reaching Home and want to delay it as long as possible. And two, see reason one again, just to emphasize the point.

Of course, this is not our conscious motive for obsessing over our potholes. We would have to have a LOT of GIGANTIC potholes—major ones, serious ones, deep ones like craters—in our driveway to justify spending the kind of time, attention, money, and energy that North Americans do on fixing them. And most of us are not in that category. The vast majority of us could never justify the resources we waste on pothole duty over and above simply turning to God and making Him the single, most important, sole aim and refuge of our life. Of course we do justify this wastage, this preoccupation with the driveway, and our delay in traveling Home. The more we have to justify our pothole improvement plan, the more baseless we can be sure it all is. God is already the most important thing in our life.

Delaying the admission and acknowledgment of this fact is endemic, built into our culture, and only painful.

How is it built into our culture? Through perfectionism. Through "not-good-enough-ism." We are obsessed with perfecting ourselves and believe that if we exist with any flaw then we are not fit to go Home. This conditioning is deeply, deeply ingrained in us. How many of us know others who in fact love us truly and perhaps unconditionally, but whose love we cannot and will not receive because deep down we are convinced that we are unworthy and undeserving? Because we have been taught that we must earn love by being good, nice, appropriate, without vice, and perfect first? So we justify our obedience to this conditioning by "working on" ourselves, and kid ourselves by saying that as soon as we've fixed the driveway up right, we'll just cruise right on into the arms of Love. We won't. We don't. We can't as long as we're committed to scarcity of Love as our perspective and bound by the association we make between our parents and God as a punitive being.

So we delay going Home, we resist going Home, even when the way is clear. We create obstacles and then justify how real those obstacles are, how our way is blocked. We keep ourselves distracted in a million ways so that we have reasons to keep fussing with the driveway. We keep our desk a mess, our finances unstable, our relationships in upheaval, our bodies over- or underweight, unhealthy and stressed, all to avoid going Home—all in protection of our belief that we are fundamentally flawed and unworthy. It is only opening to Love that can make us stop.

਼ੋ

We have a thousand ideas, beliefs, and conditionings that say higher awareness in a human being looks like specific changes in behavior, action, thought, feeling, manner, speech, et cetera, and we believe that transformation itself lies in the transformation of the quality of each of those categories; i.e., good behavior, right action, pure thought, ecstatic feeling, kind/compassionate manner, exalted speech. The discovery that the root of transformation applies to the *consciousness* of the one who is behaving, acting, thinking, feeling, mannering, and speaking, and does not necessarily impact the actions themselves, is quite revelatory.

The catch is, prior to a real transformational context being established in the practitioner, he or she is entirely focused—and in full identification with—the behavior, action, thought, feeling, manner, and speech itself, in which case there is no focus left to penetrate the question of who is behaving, acting, thinking, feeling, mannering, and speaking. This awareness, if it were available, could lead to the possibility of the practitioner realizing that *no one* is doing any of these things. If it is clear that no one is there to do anything, then the exact same behavior, actions, thoughts, feelings, manners, and speech may continue without change, even though an actual transformation has occurred.

Only after this realization (which is called "realization" because nothing actually changes—the prior reality is only observed, known, and experienced differently) has occurred and the transformation becomes the resting point of the one who has up until this time been "doing" the behaving, acting, thinking, feeling, mannering, and speaking, then these areas are also free to change, in response to the transformation being sourced from the root of the matter; that is, from the essence of the practitioner himself, instead of from the identifications of the practitioner.

At this point, those in the outside world view the "transformation" of the behavior, action, thought, feeling, manner, and speech and attempt to mimic these manifestations in their own attempts to transform themselves, without knowing the underpinnings of the entire process. This is the difference between translation and transformation and how and why so many people get hooked into a translational process instead of a transformational one. The nonlinear shift required for transformation to begin demands the abandonment of the urge to do anything with our outer manifestations except to be with them so deeply, so intimately, and with such acceptance that we are released from our identifications with them and the real work begins.

෨෯

All the efforts made toward any kind of work on self—whether that work takes the form of congratulating oneself, gaining confidence, building oneself up or tearing oneself down, beating up on oneself, judging or even hating oneself—are exactly the same. The basis of ALL this kind of work is founded in the faulty assumption that there is a self to build up, tear down, get better or worse, make progress, or fall back. There is a Self, to be sure, but it is so completely distinct from the "self" we all "work on" that these efforts are no more likely to have any impact transformationally than would changing the oil in one's car. Changing the oil in one's car may be more effective, in fact, than much of the so-called work on self that we engage.

Only Divine Influence* can illuminate the silliness of these efforts, which cannot illuminate their own futility. There must be

---

* Divine Influence - The transformative power that aligns one who is susceptible to it to the will of God. It is made tangibly available through the spiritual master or teacher.

intervention on the part of God. There must be a crack created where His Influence gets in, despite our work on ourselves. How such a crack gets created is a mystery. Perhaps the depth and persistence of longing for such intervention to occur is a good part of it. Yet it is only a miracle that produces such intervention.

ந

Transcendence as most of us imagine or desire it is rooted in getting away from, getting rid of, or not having to deal with certain realities of life, humanness, and the world. Actual transcendence is completely the opposite of this. It springs from such a total acceptance, embrace, and inclusion of all the things we would wish to be done with or avoid that most of us will never experience it because we are, at root, not interested in All, in God, in surrender to "what is." We are interested in our agenda of selective attention, awareness, and reality, which can never produce transcendence. Most spiritual seekers simply swap one set of agendas for another, practice an alternative form of selective attention, all of which only produces the same limited results in terms of actual consciousness.

Transcendence is not exclusive but inclusive. There is nothing wrong with ego and the body/mind, it is just that they must be subsumed by a bigger picture that includes them, not one which makes them wrong or tries to get rid of them. But most of us never get the bigger picture because that requires tremendous trust, and so, unconsciously, we work from the standpoint of trying to progress on the path by *excluding* elements of "what is" rather than *including* Everything in "what is."

ந

9

When one is with the Truth, regardless of what that Truth is, then one is with God. The Truth can never separate us from God. The habit of denying the Truth is so profoundly deep that we have no idea what we are really talking about when we say, "the Truth." We imagine the Truth to be something ultimately positive as opposed to negative, or beautiful as opposed to ugly, and such a box can never reveal the Truth because that's just more filtering going on.

The only reason we don't see God and experience Him in every moment is that He is not living up to our expectations. Our expectation of who, what, and how God should be, look, act, and show up in existence is the very thing that separates us from Him. To love Him is only to know that He has manifested perfectly already. Done. But then our searching is over. Then our lack of confidence has no ground. Our belief in our unworthiness and essentially flawed condition is undermined, and we stand nowhere anymore. And exactly because, if we accept this premise as the living Reality, we stand nowhere, we will know ourselves as being everywhere.

Exactly how things are is the very perfect presence of God, however twisted "the way things are" appears to the subjectively immersed mind. The kicker is that the twistedness gets projected onto God instead of the mind recognizing itself as the source of what is twisted. We might say something like, "There are people out there right now killing each other in wars. That's not God!" But instead of examining the basis—historically, culturally, psychologically—upon which we have come to our conclusions about what God is and what God is not, we just say that God is twisted. To journey from our unexamined and conditioned assumptions about the way life or God should be (which is the basis of our personal version of hell) to how life *is*, accepting it *as it is* so we can begin to work with clarity, is the essence of any real spiritual work or path.

Once we are willing to be with "what is," there is no reason for our attention ever again to contract away from all the things we now see and to localize itself in identification with any-thing. When attention no longer contracts and localizes itself, it can remain with everything. And when this occurs, all action, interaction, and behaviors arise consistent with the needs of God, the universe. The needs of All are naturally considered, and there is alignment with God's will and plan.

ða

This Work is just absolutely not what we think it is. Divine Influence does not come in the shape or form we imagine it will. Be assured that in whatever direction one is holding vigil, waiting for Benediction to arrive, it will come from the opposite direction. We can't imagine how this will take place, what the Influence actually is, or what it will look like when it arrives. We have no reference for it beyond a faint shadowy remembrance, deep in our cells, that longs for union. We have to give up every last idea of the form Help will take and simply long for it, open to it, endlessly vacant of any idea about where or what it is. But such a practice is very difficult and is challenged by everything we've ever been taught: all our conditioning, all our habits. Still, we must bang our heads and our hearts against the iron door of this practice until one day, as Rumi has put it in one of his poems, we discover that we have been knocking from inside the chamber into which we have been seeking admission.

ða

There is no such thing as an enlightened or unenlightened person. That is, there is no such thing as an enlightened or unenlightened body/mind. The body/mind just does what it does, what God has set it up to manifest as, and there is either identification with that body/mind or there is no identification. Progression on the "spiritual" path depends in part on how ruthlessly and starkly honest we can be about the body/mind and its exact manifestations, boiled down to a clear and unromantic, yet also not judgmental, view.

For instance, there are thoughts that arise within me from time to time about becoming a teacher; that is, Teacher with a capital "T". Some of these thoughts stem from a simple, passionate, and real desire to serve, while others are simply a narcissistic extension of the hero complex that has always been a prominent feature of my particular psychological structure. If you look at the thought manifestations that emanate from one who desires to be adored, worshiped, recognized for his "spiritual" status, power, or clarity, you would clearly say those thoughts/qualities are not appropriate to anyone who truly has anything to offer in terms of serving liberation of others. What we need, we think, is one who is always truly selfless, has pure thoughts, beautiful feelings. By looking for and perhaps finding and following such a one, we can (and many, many do) cripple our understanding of the dynamics of liberation to the point that we spend the rest of our lives, and maybe many more lives, attempting to mimic the goodness or perfectness or ideals we attribute to a liberated one instead of ever coming within a million miles of the perfect release of self that accompanies the abandonment of any idea about what liberation looks like, acts like, or is like, and realizing eventually that we are that very liberation already.

Put liberation first, change follows. Put change first, liberation flees. But we must put change first over and over before we can glimpse the futility of making changes and eventually relinquish changing ourselves as the path we cling to. We were born into a world, and into a family most likely, that taught us from the very beginning that if we were going to be loved, if we were going to survive, then we damn well better be something other than what we appeared as at two years of age, or whenever we first got the message. The need to not be who we are, to not see or admit exactly who we are, is precisely the departure point to which we must retrace our steps and pick up the work of becoming naturally and wholly human. To be exactly who we are—to see and admit who we are—is 99.9 percent of the spiritual quest. The .1 percent of the work that's left to do after that is the most important, significant, and mind-blowing part, and this, fortunately, gets done by God.

&#10086;

One day we shall have to stop thinking "ourselves" into existence. This activity of making ourselves up as creatures of limited form is not sustainable. It is a doing that one day will exhaust us into non-doing, and this is what we sense will be our death. Indeed, it will be the death of the limited and boundaried self, but in mis-identification with this small self we do not see the Self that will survive this death.

The mis-identification comes from an attachment to a limited area of concern. We strive to make changes to that which is within our area of concern—with whatever we call "us." Most people's area of concern is within the area bounded by their skin. This also includes whatever affects, supports, hampers, or comes in contact with the fleshy, solid body. The area of concern is made to include those things with which the body is associated: one's family, house, possessions, business, mate, et cetera. When we work to change anything within this strictly defined area of identification or concern, we are involved in what is called a translational process. Translation is the countless number of unlimited and unending changes that we make to the content within the perceived area of the self.

A transformational process is a process in which the imagined border, not the content, of the area of concern is obliterated, creating ambiguity, fluidity, and even wonder about where one actually begins and ends, even though the content, characteristics, and features within the previous area of identification have not "transformed" at all.

The transformational process does not concern itself with the content within the boundary that borders self but involves relaxing the fixed nature of this boundary and then surrendering it completely. There is a fixed amount of atmospheric pressure that inhabits the space of one's defined area of identification. The smaller the space, the greater the pressure. Most forms of disease, discomfort, neurosis, and agitation are just the manifestation of increased atmospheric pressure—the atmosphere of the chosen size of self. The more that area is expanded, the lower the pressure, which produces manifestations such as lightness, humor, spontaneity, joy, love. When there are no edges to the area of identification, there is no identification at all possible and a no-pressure state is realized. This no-pressure state delivers a clarity and purpose, intention and necessity which can, with the proper guidance, be the basis of a real spiritual practice.

꙳

A useful metaphor for the appropriate way to work with one's unwanted personality or psychological manifestations is the way in which karate experts are trained to break a board in half. The focus for one who is endeavoring to break a wooden board is not on the board itself, but on a point quite beyond it. An expert in breaking boards is moving his or her hand from a point above the board to a destination which is down near the floor. The hand is bound for that point "beyond," and on the way to that point the hand clears the board as an obstacle.

If the mind of the practitioner is intent on clearing the obstacle instead of simply being inspired by the true goal (the point beyond), there is the likelihood that not only will the hand be stopped by the manifestation, but the hand is likely to become damaged in the process when it slams into the thing which the mind has made more solid by its focus upon it.

Straight battle with the manifestation itself can be dangerous and harmful, because an obstacle or manifestation does not hold the necessary force or power it requires to go beyond itself. If it did, it would transform itself. It would, in fact, not exist in its current form. The only possibility for its transformation lies in allowing an outside source to deliver it to a higher order. To fight with a particular manifestation is to reduce the available Influence for the transformation of that manifestation to the level of the obstacle itself (because the focus is there), thereby short-circuiting the possibility of going beyond it. We must be inspired by something beyond the manifestation and let the inspiration from this source wage the battle of transforming particular manifestations for us.

We cannot do it ourselves because we are nothing but a servant to whatever our attention is on. If one puts his or her attention on the problem or the obstacle, on the manifestation itself (even if it's with the intention of ridding oneself of it), one is actually just lending it the strength and ability to persist. If one puts his or her attention on God, one is creating an open channel through which miracles can, and do, occur by God's hand.

☙

The "blocks" we experience are blocks only because we are focused on them. Since they are always there when we turn our attention towards them, we mistakenly assume they are also there when our attention is not on them. It is like someone who becomes obsessed with why pinching himself hurts, and then keeps pinching himself over and over to try and get to the bottom of why it hurts so much, instead of just realizing that if he stops pinching himself the problem of hurting is not solved but dissolved.

If one looks at one's own eyes in the mirror, inseparable to that action is the phenomenon of the eyes looking back at the eyes that are looking at them. If one keeps staring at these eyes, wondering if they will ever look away, the conclusion one will draw is that they never do look away. If there is a growing impatience for the eyes in the mirror to stop looking at oneself, such that one never stops looking at those eyes because one wants them to stop looking at himself, it is obvious what kind of madness would result. But the madness includes the deep-seated belief that because those eyes are always looking at us in our experience, they are always looking at us, even when our attention is elsewhere. We cannot experience the absence of our "problems"; therefore, our experience always reinforces that we have a problem.

☙

There is a context shift that is essential to this Process that is distinct from all other shifts of context. The standard shift being pedaled at growth workshops, or even to an extent by therapy, is that of going from being a spectator at a tennis match to being a player on the court. So instead of judging, criticizing, or envying the play from the stands, we are actually playing; playing the game. We have then moved out of the passive victim position, who has things happen to him or her, into the active participant position, who is making things happen, expressing himself, taking charge of his life.

This feels like a significant shift, and it is. But the contextual shift that reaches the heart is when one becomes the ball. Then the game is playing us. One could not be more integral to the action, to the game, but it would be impossible to win or lose from this perspective because the ball is so intimately involved in the play that it is inseparable from it. Occasionally, it may even wind up in the stands, but it doesn't matter. Wherever the game goes, there it is. So there is no relationship to the game. It, in effect, is the game, which makes it impossible to be at the effect of the game, its outcomes, its ups and downs. Ordinarily we believe that to transcend the game we must distance ourselves from it, stand back from it, which is how we wind up in the stands as a spectator with no control.

The path to transcendence is to be so integrally involved in the play that, although we are completely without control, we can no longer be affected in any way by the game. Any boxer knows this. If you want to avoid getting knocked out by your opponent, you don't run away, because where will you go? There is no escape in the ring. But if you get close enough to the opponent, he can no longer strike you down. Remain at arm's length from life and you are setting yourself up to get flattened every time. Get as close as you can to life and you will become undefeatable.

&

Imagine that you had no feeling skin on your body as a sense organ and you left the house to run an errand on an extremely windy day. Walking down the street looking up, you suddenly—concurrent with a rushing sound in your ears—see the trees swaying wildly to and fro. Other objects in your field of vision also start moving and dancing around randomly. A piece of paper mysteriously flies across the street. A flag dances in the air. In an instant your hat is snatched from your head and races away from you and you chase it. You're walking to the store and before getting there you check your wallet to make sure you have enough money for milk and suddenly, without warning, a fifty dollar bill is snatched by an unseen force from your hand and spirited away into a crowd of shoppers. Your money is gone. What cruel act of God can this be, you wonder? What confusion to live in a world where an unfelt, unknown, and unpredictable force moves objects at random, without warning or reason.

This is our situation. Except the "skin" we are living without is a mechanism that can feel and sense the movement of spirit that, like wind, is not visible to the eye, but is clearly communicating about the movements and unseen causes of Reality in its own language. If this language is known—if we are sensitive to it—all the things that used to confuse us, confound us, prompt us to make up stories about God, cause us misery, and surprise us, would suddenly make perfect sense, not only to our minds but to our very body and being. We would be so connected to spirit that the unseen force, acting on all facets of existence, would allow us the "inside scoop" on the what and why of Everything. There would be nothing unknown to us, no basis on which we would forge expectations that relegated the realm of the possible to the impossible, and therefore no angst, no pain, no struggle when the so-called "impossible" just continued to happen, over and over. The happenings of the universe would no longer be consistently issued the labels of being for us or against us. We would instead just see that the way things go is lawfully the only way they can go and what happens in the universe is simply not about us at all.

❧

Impeccable integrity means never losing Context, never being swayed by the dominance of one "I" over and above another, never identifying with one part to the exclusion of Context and acting according to the dictates of that part as if it were the only authority or truth. But this kind of identification is the default mode of just about everyone all the time. One center, one "I" at a time, running the ship, steering the boat for a few seconds before another "I" hits it over the head and takes control of the wheel, just because it happened to be a little stronger in that moment. The centers and the I's war for control just like animals do in nature. It's survival of the strongest. And these I's that are always winning control of us have tremendous passion and energy, but zero vision—absolutely no idea of God, of Love, of service, of integrity. They cannot by their very nature know God.

Basic integrity can be learned, absorbed, and achieved with a good deal of practice and by hanging around the right influences long enough. Total integrity is much more radical and requires a level of practice that burns the practitioner into nothing so that there is no one for the I's to battle for control over. The I's are still there, they can still war with each other, but the literal battleground is gone, and they can no longer do any harm because they have no tangent point through which they can intersect with the world.

❧

Our situation as individuals in this culture who have taken a fancy to the fad of ridding ourselves of ego is like that of a man standing alone in a bare room with a big wad of two-day-old

19

gum stuck firmly on the middle of his back. He cannot reach this particular spot with either hand, and there is nothing else in the room. He jumps up and down violently for a while, to no avail. Eventually, he starts rolling on the floor or up against the walls, and still the gum doesn't get removed; it only starts stringing itself from place to place, leaving sticky trails all over the room. When things really get bad, and the floor and walls are covered, he invites other people with gum wads on their backs into his room to have a "group" or workshop so they can mix the gooey strands of their predicament together. The members of the "group" never show their backs, because they never remain in relationship long enough to actually trust one another, so they never see the source of their problem and are unable to help each other. The entanglement just gets worse and worse and no one can figure it out. Finally, everyone goes home, leaving the host alone with the whole disaster. Now he has not only his own mess, but remnants and strands of everyone else's.

Then there is a knock on the door. The man looks out and sees some stranger who says, "Look, I can't clean up this mess, but I know where the mess is coming from, and I can remove the source. You'll have to do your own cleaning up here, but at least you won't keep making the mess over and over."

The man says, "Oh, thank God!" with an enthusiastic smile which vanishes as soon as the stranger says, "Okay, turn around."

"What? Turn around? Hah! That's a good one. I haven't turned around since I was six months old. I learned that lesson a long time ago, pal. You're not going to get me on that one. Turn around, indeed. What do you take me for?"

"No, really. Turn around. It's the only way I can help."

"Hey, I'm willing to do anything you ask to get this situation handled *except* turn around."

"Oh. Okay . . . well, call me when you're ready to turn around."

And out the stranger goes, making his rounds to all who will let him in the door, making his pitch like a vacuum cleaner salesman, but with a much lower rate of success with his door-to-door strategy, because what he is selling is the original Vacuum, and almost no one ever buys, because from ego's perspective, it really sucks!

❧

Tantric practice is the ability to align oneself with the Work value inherent in any situation, circumstance, or relationship. Another way of saying this is that tantric practice is about using everything and anything as a fuel source to feed God. Lust, greed, anger, fear, sentimentality—all are only sockets in the wall that we can plug into as a fuel source. Because humans have been given this thing called free will, it's up to us what we do with the live wires we have once we are plugged into a socket. Our habit is to take the free hot leads we're holding and shove them right back into the same socket, creating a loop in which the source of the energy feeds only itself and evolution is short-circuited—evolution, in fact, becomes literally impossible—because the energy has no means of serving anything other than its current condition. Shoving the leads back into the original fuel source occurs when we identify with the current source *as* ourselves. The pure raw energy of anger, for instance, becomes, "*I* am angry." It is all a matter of where we are putting our attention.

When we begin to learn about the Work,* learn to Remember God and consider the Divine, one day, while holding the leads, a miracle occurs; even though we are plugged into something like fear or lust, we find out that by considering God in that moment the free leads make a connection to the Divine and conduct the energy to God. Then God gets fed.

This is exactly what a human being is meant to do. It is the highest possibility and perfect destiny of a human being: to become a transformational agent in service to God by plugging into these raw and gross energy forms which God cannot access in any other way except through us; to not become identified with them—thereby not feeding back into them—and deliver this raw material to the Lord for His purposes. To be just a delivery agent. Like a postman.

But imagine a postman who in the course of his job of delivering the mail imagined that all the mail in the bag was his! That's what we do. All of these energies come to us, and we never think that maybe they haven't been addressed to us at all and we're supposed to just pass them along. We get a package and we rip it open, let the whole thing out, take a bath in it, get obsessed by it, wear it on our head, or put it on the mantlepiece in our living room. We're stealing! Really. It was never meant for us. It's all God's. It's all addressed to Him. But we adopt it, take it in, and God starves. And when God starves, we don't get fed. Well, we get fed on one level—our bellies get fatter, our heads get wider—but our souls start to wither, shrink, and dry up.

We must fundamentally rewire our entire structure, create a completely new body of habits over a long period of time and practice, before we can even begin to know experientially the truth of this for

---

* The Work - Used in many spiritual traditions to refer to the objective Work of God in which human beings are called to participate.

ourselves. Once we see that it is really true, that this is really how it is, then our zeal to come into right relationship with it all will blossom. The thing is, what we get back from God when we deliver what is truly His to Him is beyond compare to whatever we have sacrificed through non-identification. But, of course, what we get from God has to go back to Him as well, and that takes another significant amount of time and practice to discover. Eventually, if we persist, the supremacy of the Law of sacrifice reveals itself as the final and ultimate law of existence.

The fundamental stumbling block for Westerners is the taboos that prevent any relationship at all to these unrefined energy sources, to the sockets. The entire New Age movement is nothing more than an offshoot of puritanical influences which teach that only particular energies are acceptable to be accessing at all. The nice, peaceful, calm, blissful, loving kinds of feelings. These kinds of feelings are paupers in terms of Work value, and trying to get food for God out of them is like trying to get human contact off the Internet.

They are constructed entirely out of conceptual energies, which are the most weak of forces for work because, like inert substances on the chart of elements, their molecular rings are complete. There is no room for any other substance to interact with them; there is no way to cause a reaction with them in which the components of which they are made come apart and the energy composing them is released for the formation of new substances. So because all these "nice" feelings are conceptual only, no one on any New Age path ever gets anywhere but exactly where they started from.

Other spiritual paths, especially those of the Eastern traditions, make varying degrees of use of the substances and elements that have true power and true Work potential—tantric spiritual practice being the path which is most daring in its utilization of the strongest and most potent sources of fuel. The problem is, of course, that the more powerful the agents one taps into, the more skilled and trained one must be to use them without getting burned or blown up; thus, the warnings that authentic Teachers in tantric practice always deliver before accepting anyone into any degree of confidence about the Teaching and its associated secrets.

As Westerners, one of our first tasks on the path is simply to retrain ourselves to be able to access these vital energy sources. Some groups in North American culture do have access to these energies, but lack the education necessary to be able to direct them into the service of spiritual growth. The increasingly independent teen group and the African-American population are generalized examples of some who still have a passionate feeling relationship to life even though they live in a world that increasingly values and rewards only restraint, intellectual property, and control. Without proper guidance and mentoring, members of such groups often wind up as puppets to waves of passion, lost and out of control, thrown about by the whim of the forces of nature within them. This leaves them with the sense that life itself is cruel, an anarchy that they must tolerate for the duration of their mortality; and from that perspective, with no other possibility in sight, they angrily submit to serving this seemingly senseless arrangement by abandoning consciousness to the lowest expressions of God's passions.

These are the two camps that North Americans fall into: blocked from access to energy, or able to access energy but uneducated in its appropriate use. Most therapies and growth modalities focus on one or the other of these "problems," but do not address the other. Encounter groups, free sex "tantra" crash courses, drug experimentation, and occultism are examples of movements that get in touch with these energies without respect for the proper education required to use them effectively. Most types of counseling and psychotherapy, the currently popular enneagram groups, many Gurdjieff group off-shoots, and all psychologically-based study modalities are examples of methods that never properly mine the sources of fuel that are required for any kind of real movement on the path, though they are rich with data. Both of these cultural stumbling blocks must be adequately acknowledged, addressed, and provided for in any work which attempts to bring the Westerner into a relationship with the right and true use of human life as a transformational opportunity.

&#42;

The spiritual student is in an amusement park. All the buzz and the rhetoric surrounds how to win the giant stuffed Panda. It's so rare that one can win one of the big stuffed animals; it almost never happens. In the park there are many other students all trying to win the Panda, sharing legends and telling stories about those who have won them. So that's the goal for all these seekers. And every so often it happens. You see someone walking around with one of the coveted prizes and he or she is revered, respected, admired; all heads turn for the winner of the giant Panda. The bear is so obvious, so triumphant in the arms of the owner, that he can even feign great humility, but only because he knows the sheer size of the bear will do all the bragging for him. He seems like a victor, but the moment he stops playing the games, thinking he now has the greatest prize, and passes outside the gates of the amusement park, God himself aches with pain for the one who has settled for the booby prize.

There is another winner in the park who also somehow achieves the Panda but walks around with it for only a few minutes before an invisible force draws him near a sideshow barker who stands alone in a little booth, observing the passing multitudes. Almost no one pays any attention or stops to investigate. But this rare individual with the bear, for some inexplicable reason, stops and walks forward. The barker bends and whispers something into the ear of the Panda winner, who passes the prize slowly over the counter, bewildered himself as to why he would part with it. Then the barker smiles tenderly and hands the winner something indistinguishably small, which he places into his pocket before walking away.

If you ducked behind a tent just in time to intercept this person before he left the fairgrounds, and you divulged to him that you had seen the whole transaction and begged with utmost urgency and sincerity to know what he had traded the Panda for, he just might glance cautiously right and left, measure you with a steady gaze to weigh the longing of your soul and, if it were sufficient, remove a hand from his pocket and open it to let you see one small sharp thorn.

The rest of the world will pass right by this winner from now on, never knowing of the treasure gained by this one in the most secret game on the carnival grounds. This one may continue to play all the other games, but will never again play to win, because he has already won the only prize worth living for: a way to always and forever Remember.

The sideshow barker is the true Teacher, the one who takes away what seems to be the grand prize in return for something of eternal value. The one who hands out the Pandas to those who have a lucky day at ring toss, however, is nothing more than a businessman who needs occasional winners to keep a steady stream of suckers in line at his stand.

ह

Everyone talks and proceeds and practices as if consciousness is something "out there" that we must get or obtain. Consciousness *is* us. It is *in* the body, resident there. It is simply that we are keeping it confined to a very limited version of ourselves. It is only the tension we hold in our body (physical, psychic, emotional) that holds this consciousness *in;* limits it to a finite area. This is the exact meaning of self-referencing, when we only allow our consciousness to roam in an exclusive area, barriered by these tensions. When the tensions are released, it is like taking down prison walls. We know we have walls, but we think the walls are keeping what we need from reaching us, when exactly the opposite is true. The walls are keeping what we are from reaching Everything. So when those tensions are dropped, consciousness is released and moves outward, from ourselves as the source, to Everything, including Everything, and surrounding Everything. The moment our consciousness expands we become that which it has reached, and the old view of what we were is shattered, undermined; and in such a moment we know freedom.

&

The first thing that happens if we are ever successful in building a store of core energy is that it gets immediately stolen by our egoic tendencies, which become so big and fully animated that it may feel like the difference between riding a bicycle and driving a Porsche. In the sports car, losing control is suddenly much easier to do, and we might have a few accidents before we learn to be cautious of the power at our fingertips. The more energy one manages to accumulate through Work, the bigger and more animated the old habits will appear, until it is finally impossible to deny, avoid, or escape dealing with them, though we will try for a long time. Our egoic tendencies may get so big and be so horrific for us to look at— so contrary to our self-image, which we were able to keep in place with buffers when ego had little energy at its disposal—that some form of suicide may cross the mind as an alternative to looking at the underbelly or unmasked face of our persona.

But once this face is seen and these parts of oneself admitted, surrendering the ego identity becomes more attractive because we can clearly see that it is not as wonderful as we were telling ourselves and that, in fact, it is the cause of great pain to ourselves and others. We are brought into a humility from which protection of our personality is not as compelling a proposition because we see all our parts, not just the self-flattering ones.

There are two options once the Truth starts becoming apparent. One is to self-destruct out of self-hatred in reaction to what is now seen, and the other is to be pierced by the Truth as it is, even though it is distasteful, frightening, or threatening. If one manages to stomach the terror of the second option, there will be a grand shake-up of the whole ego complex. It will come apart, and some kind of reordering will have to occur. Through the acceptance of "what is," the old boundaries are weakened or even totally obliterated, no longer able to wall out what ego was strategically dissociating itself from. When all that we were previously denying is let in, we stop protecting who and what it is we think we are, and a mysteriousness might enter the picture. We may start to feel that we do not know exactly who we are anymore, or may even in moments be unable to find anything that we are not, and we may begin to think we are going mad or losing touch with "reality." We are, in fact, just beginning to open to Reality if this happens. If the knack of this openness to all of "what is" takes hold and one dives more deeply in, one comes to experience the original face—the face that is without character, without persona—and at this point one has truly "lost face." Losing face is the only possibility for a transformed life. The beginning of transformation is to lose the personal and merge with the Universal, with Everything.

❧

When we think the Work is about becoming different, our effort to effect change in ourselves comes from the same faulty and ignorant foundation of understanding as all the rest of our ego-centered pursuits, and we are doomed to fall into the same mechanical behavior that accompanies that veil of ignorance. The *by-product* of the Work is becoming different. The Work itself is about surrender. Surrender handles the desire to become different, which is always ego driven before surrender occurs. After surrender, the necessity to be different will arise from what one sees and knows rather than from what one does not see and does not know. There is nothing we can do or even need to do to become different.

❧

While walking over a long bridge today with a friend, I laughed, struck by the absurdity of the mind's idea of spiritual work: how it thinks it needs to change itself or something else in order for the Divine to exist. After the laugh my friend said, "What?," and then I said, "Ego is simply not a problem." And she said, "Wouldn't it be a problem for someone who thinks it's a problem?" I replied, "Yes, of course, but once the person realized it isn't a problem they would realize that it isn't a problem not because of some understanding they were finally able to gain but because it was never a problem, even when they thought it was."

The bridge we were walking over is probably a hundred and fifty feet above the water and half a mile long, made up of hundreds or thousands of tons of concrete and steel. From our vantage point walking on it we could see a lot of bridge, but only the surface, high above the water. The underside was completely invisible to us. Looking over the edge of the bridge to the water below was dizzying. To be on this huge, massive thing suspended in the air was frightening; the mind could easily imagine it collapsing at any moment. But mind doesn't see the immense concrete pillars and steel scaffolding which are networked perfectly under the bridge to support it. Because we don't see the underpinnings—the foundation on which the bridge is built—fear arises.

It is the same with ego. Mind only sees the surface of who we are. When we add the awareness of what ego is based on, resting on, and founded in, it no longer appears as a problem that needs to be addressed. So rather than attempting to destroy the "bridge," or feeling compelled to avoid using it, our work is about discovering the Reality of its support, which we accomplish through enquiry, play, trust, and curiosity; not destruction or avoidance. But we're trained in destruction and avoidance, not in openness and curiosity with regard to ourselves.

So how do we help those who feel unsupported? It isn't by giving them a technical description of what's under the bridge and calling them names for not realizing the perfect design of the structure. It's by giving them an *experience* of being supported. Extending kindness, generosity, and compassion toward those who live in fear is what communicates the Reality of this Divine design by which we are held. This approach, slowly, over time, allows the fearful ones to begin to rest in themselves as they are.

≈

The first thing that must happen on the spiritual path is that we realize or admit that we cannot beat the pain we are in. That requires a great deal of self-observation and honesty and courage. Then we may start to admit our separative tendencies and the degree of pain they bring to ourselves and to others. If we do this, we start to come out of denial about what we are and how we are. We get a little bit of objectivity about our current condition and gain a "you are here" point on the map. Once we know where we're starting from, we can begin for the first time to make use of the map to navigate towards the Truth.

If we work with this first stage diligently, we then progress to the second stage, in which we begin to willingly access new parts of ourselves, of what it means to be human, and to live as a multidimensional, somewhat balanced human being no longer confined to only one or two modes of behavior. We begin to reclaim our feeling selves, updating into adulthood, and melt the rigidity of the frightened child into some degree of participation and functionality in the world that is outside of the previous constraints of our comfort zone. This is the realm of almost all healing, psychological, therapeutic, and self-improvement work. Those who have a hunger for God and for Reality usually take level two work to an extreme and make great progress at that level. They may even become highly successful or powerful in the world and forget for many years or decades about their original thirst for the Truth. Or, if they do not forget, they pour their passion into obsessive self-improvement, and indeed their self does improve. The more such a person works at this level, the more ripe they become for level three work, even though they may feel increasingly empty and unfulfilled by their current lives. In fact, the more empty and the more unsatisfied they find themselves by this level of work, by their inability to rearrange their psychological structure and achieve self-perfection, the more they are prone to discovering a whole new game, a whole new Context which is the beginning of a life of service in God.

The third level is the level at which transformation occurs. The third level begins when, through a living Teacher, the Influence of the Divine creates an impression on the soul that sets it ringing at a frequency that is completely destructive—the same way that, in an earthquake, the vibrational rate of the unleashed force makes it impossible for any structure to remain in place because it is so wild, so radically unstable. What feels like a radical lack of stability in the moment in which it is experienced is in actuality a profound fluidity, the same fluidity which earthquake survivors have described witnessing on the surface of the planet during a quake: that solid earth looked and behaved like a liquid. In the face of this shock, this reference for Divinity, the entirety of all the parts which have been reclaimed, worked on, perfected, polished, and examined by the seeker are suddenly abandoned all at once, as a whole, in a single moment of surrender that renders one absolutely distinct from all the manifestations which were the previous, complete, and exclusive focus of attention. It is the discovery of *who* one really is, entirely distinct from *what* one is. It is the discovery of Context over and above content.

Working with a Teacher creates a very refined intelligence, since His living manifestations undermine all the strategies of the mind and force confrontation with what seem to be the contradictions which the mind perceives. When the mind must cross-reference constantly and create a refined quality of distinctions that account for the Reality of the Teacher, a type of intelligence is established as a framework for practice that is far beyond the black-and-white-box type of living and coping strategies that we normally rely on. Such an intelligence is capable of sustaining a relationship to the True and incomprehensible mystery which Reality is. In diving into this mystery, things become more and more humorous as the old mode of "working on self" becomes obviously absurd; yet the habit of engaging in this mode has not disappeared even though one has essentially disconnected from it. In this stage, old habits, behaviors, concerns, and psychological tendencies may continue to be engaged, but there will be a vast perceived distance between these "habits" and who one actually is. This is the stage where conscious suffering occurs. We begin to see and suffer that which, in the still present personality, does not reflect, resonate with, and abide in the Divine. In this stage one feels immense gratitude and benediction coming from the Divine but cannot yet gesture back with enlightened action, speech, and conscious sacrifice. The very condition of having seen one's true Self projected against the unconscious habits of ego identification creates a heat, a friction, and a remorse which is so powerful, so intense, that the practitioner will be re-shaped, re-built, the nervous system re-wired, and the Heart literally forged from the pain of the discrepancy between the two.

During this period the disciple may feel that it is necessary or important that he or she become radically different in a way that honors and expresses the immensity and profundity of what they have glimpsed in consciousness. This may likely take the form of a felt necessity for more external change; i.e., how one acts, what one does. The motivation to "be different" is now more powerful than ever, backed by the force of Love and the Divine. What the practitioner finds, however, is that any progression in the realm of making a change is always stalled and blocked by willful efforts and that only surrender to what they are and have been all along can work the magic that is required.

After a period of trying to wrestle these unresonant parts into alignment with consciousness, they are surrendered to, similar to what had occurred in the first stage of the path, but this time, as the disciple surrenders to his separative tendencies, the tendencies themselves are filled with the breath of the Divine, or divinized, consecrated, as they are, and all of these previously destructive tendencies are re-ordered internally to become expressions of the Divine. This leads to an impossible paradox in which the manifestations of the devotee, regardless of appearances, are imbued with a radiance, a joy and lightness which is attractive, even irresistible if not also confounding, to others. This complete assumption of all of the devotee's tendencies into the chamber of the Heart, into the Heart of Communion, is the marriage of heaven and earth in human form; the highest potential of a human being, the frontier of evolution for the human race.

**ॐ**

We live in a valley that is surrounded by mountains. We never think to push on them because they look so substantial, so real, so solid, so immovable. But if we finally do, we find them to be like inflatable props or just backdrops airbrushed on silk, no more permanent, immovable, or impervious than the air we breathe. We beg and pray for the kind of freedom that knows no bounds and is not confined by the constructs of our belief systems, but the terror of having nothing of substance we can use as an excuse to stay where we are and use to guard ourselves against the unknown keeps us pretending our constructs are real.

People are afraid of what they really are, which is space. The opposite of space is the victim. The victim lives in the illusion of being surrounded on all sides, bounded by circumstances. The victim uses circumstances to try and combat the terrorizing Truth of endless space, of infinite freedom.

For the spiritual practitioner there comes the time when even all the cherished ideals, ideas, and concepts about what spirituality actually is, which were necessary and helpful at a certain stage of practice, must be completely and totally abandoned. Having no idea about what Influence actually is or where it actually comes from is the only way to access the level of Influence which can completely undermine the mind's grip on a life founded in illusion and ignorance. Nothing escapes God. Everything is God, including all the things we habitually wall out and put a fence around as unworthy of our attention, participation, and love because, we believe, the things on the other side of the fence are "not God." There is nothing that is not God. When that Reality penetrates fully, the mind cannot withstand the hurricane of realization that blows every idea about what Reality actually is right off the map. Everything is God.

ॐ

We must surrender to what we Are already. We must stop guessing and wondering at what we would be if we were truly ourselves, and *be* that. Surrendering to ourselves is no different from surrendering to the entire Universe. If we surrender to ourselves, we will know ourselves *as* the entire Universe. Relationship to ourselves *is* relationship to Everything.

Why? Because we are IT. Consistent with the childhood game of tag, we have been deeply, deeply conditioned, far beyond our conscious awareness, to not be IT. If one is IT in the sleeping world, they are the loser, the outsider, alone, left holding the bag. No one wants to be IT. Well, the truth is, we are IT, no matter what. Everyone is IT. There is another world, this one actually, where to be IT is the most sublime ecstasy, privilege, and glorious wonder possible. Are we willing to be IT forever with no take-backs, no hand-offs, no one else to dump it on? Are we willing to say, "I am the one for the job"? Are we willing to be one hundred percent responsible for what we already are and will always be?

ॐ

When we read spiritual literature or are exposed to descriptions of some facet of spiritual practice, it is like coming upon a door. A door we have never seen. A possible passageway to our transformation. The tendency of mind is to enter into a stream of random associations provoked by the appearance of the door; perhaps begin debating its usefulness, origin, or history; spend time examining its properties; or even praise and glorify it. In our preoccupation with the door's characteristics, we stand before it pretending that we have entered the space which the door defines without realizing that we have not entered anywhere new. We haven't left our mental prison yet. We are still exactly in the same space. We enter into this kind of activity with such a door because the mind cannot do anything in relationship to it. The door has no handle on the side which faces the mind. We cannot open it with any degree of intellectual facility or will. The secret to right relationship to such a door is to lean on it with the full commitment of our body and spirit. Because any door to transformation is a door which opens outward to the new, never inward toward what we already are, we must approach the door and put ourselves off balance by surrendering our full weight to it, with no holdout, no way of catching ourselves or protecting ourselves from a fall should the door ever open of its own accord. It is the Divine itself that opens this door, and the Divine responds to the fully surrendered weight of one who presses her longing, her intention, her patience and devotion against it.

❧

There can only be one reason to want to do anything at all about ego—that reason being if we think we are ego. When it becomes absolutely obvious that one is not ego, the desire or need to work with it, do anything about it, handle it, or get rid of it just vanishes, and there is, for the first time, the deepest ease. The desire or need to do anything at all with or about ego is ego. Ego is a crazy person pinching himself and becoming fascinated and endlessly involved in the sensation of the self-inflicted pain. The process of trying or wanting to do something about the pain becomes a safety zone, a security blanket that one never lets go of to avoid Nothingness. Because of this payoff, the person never just stops pinching himself. Instead, he generates endless activity that seems to be dedicated to wanting the pain to cease but is, in reality, devotion to the avoidance of Reality, of Truth, of the true Self. We've been so conditioned to believe we are not enough—that we're incomplete—that to accept into our own mouths the declaration "I am Whole!" is almost impossible for anyone of this culture. Ego just is, and can be left completely alone to do what it does best. Ego can never and does not need to change. One simply recognizes that one is not that. In fact, one is nothing at all. Ego exists, but not as "I".

ॐ

There are two types of math: the math of the masses and the math of the mystic. The math of the masses is based on multiplication, and secondarily uses division, addition, and subtraction. But each of these devices is the same. They all produce some form of answer. They all produce a final tally or result. Multiplication is the process of making something out of something. And what has that given us? Pollution, trip cancellation insurance, the Internet, bra strap headbands (they actually exist), Preparation H.

The math of the mystic requires the abandonment of multiplication and is based on a higher and quite rarely applied mathematical procedure called simplification. To simplify is to make nothing out of something. If simplification is practiced diligently, one eventually arrives at the point where there is nothing at all. And what a grand moment that is! Because when there is nothing at all, then one can marvel in the Divine as it makes something out of nothing.

≀❧

All of life and evolution rests on the Law of sacrifice.* The understanding that who and what we currently are will always be sacrificed—that is, change or evolve into something else, no matter how much we want to hold on to its current form—is the only thing that allows us to sustain a life of spiritual practice.

We must arrive at the conclusion that it is better to consciously sacrifice than it is to *be* sacrificed. Either we elegantly give up what we have and are in any given moment in which this is appropriate, or we hang on and the Law itself selects a random pound of flesh and extracts it from us as the payment which is due. It's kind of like being permanently strapped into a race car with a perpetual tank of fuel and the gas pedal bolted full throttle to the floor. The question is not speed forward into the unknown or do not speed forward into the unknown but, rather, steer or don't steer. We do have the freedom to sacrifice voluntarily, which is all that spiritual life is: the art of voluntary, rather than forced, sacrifice.

Once we have sacrificed a thing, it is in our best interest to forget the sacrifice was made as soon as possible and go on. To bring attention to the fact that one has sacrificed—to boast about it, show it off —is to simply take back what has been sacrificed, and the gesture is nullified in direct proportion to the degree that it is worn as a badge. These sacrifices over time will build a substance in the body that might be called intention, and intention is the form of currency we

---

* The Law of sacrifice - The sacrificial nature of all elements of existence, according to which everything is food for everything else. The Law can be consciously lived.

must accumulate to pay for Attention from God. We declare the depth of our desire to know God through the demonstration of what we are willing to give up in return and how quiet we are willing to keep about it.

The Law of sacrifice says, if you're willing to consciously give up what is most dear to you, you will be presented with something even more dear. That sounds great, and it is great, because it always works. But the catch is, you can never stop participating in the Law once you have established a relationship to it. If you keep getting things that are even more dear than you can possibly imagine, you will have to sacrifice those things also. And when you do, things that are even more unimaginably sublime will appear, and so on. It is a game of spiritual chicken.

When we hit the point at which we've taken as much as we can, and we want to opt out, there are two possibilities. One is to run, in which case the Divine runs after us to get the final payment it requires in return for what has been given so far. And it always catches up, even if we find a very elaborate hiding place.

In the second scenario, we've taken as much as we can take but instead of attempting to alleviate the stress of the process, we opt out of *identification* with the one whom the stress seems to be impacting. Then we experience the most distinct, strange, and inexplicable revelation possible. We see that everything we ever thought we were was only a shadow and that everything we truly are is the Process itself. In this moment of realizing that we are actually the Process itself, or Everything, we will, according to the Law, be required to give Everything up, and then we will get Everything back in the same instant, all in a framework which constitutes no time and takes up no space. This getting Everything and giving up of Everything spontaneously, continuously, and infinitely occurs from then on as the perfect representation of the Law of sacrifice at its highest level.

৯

The trick is to contextualize whatever it is that arises in awareness instead of identifying with it to the exclusion of the awareness of other things. To place any thoughts, sensations, feelings, phenomena, or behavior in Context is the aim of the Work. Because the habit of exclusive identification with these things is so strong, and our reactions to this identification so entrenched, it is virtually impossible to make any headway into contextualizing them properly, and thereby transforming them, unless we have been practicing resting in that Context under less challenging circumstances. This is the purpose and value of meditation. Meditation is the time when we should be working very hard to establish ourselves in true Context with the hope that one day the same vast Context will be available to us even in the midst of the habit of contracting around our self-phenomena in daily life. But this is not the way we are trained in Western culture to deal with those manifestations which are unpleasant to us or that we want to change.

People think they can work on specific areas of manifestation. This takes the form of focusing on them, and focusing on them is exactly the problem. When we make them a problem and focus on them to work with them or get rid of them, we narrow our attention and make the process of subsuming these manifestations in true Context impossible. We must open our attention around the manifestation and embrace it, contain it, and surround it; drown it within this spaciousness. When we do this, if we are doing it properly, the thing that we thought was such a big deal is suddenly put in its rightful Context, and it becomes very small and insignificant. But ours is a culture which sells the idea that you can lose body fat in only certain areas of your body by focusing on them with particular exercises or subjecting them to forms of machinery or ingesting certain particular foods. We have even invented a name for the "problem"—we call it "cellulite"—even though any exercise physiologist will tell you that a "weight problem," even if it appears to be localized, can only be handled by adapting lifestyle behaviors that affect our total body fat percentage. Then the whole body is affected by these new practices. Similarly, we can train ourselves to turn to Context, to rest in Context in all of life, and that in turn will naturally address any areas of our lives which require specific corrections, adjustments, or realignment to the Truth.

&

All seeking of liberation or enlightenment is only part of the drama of self. There is either continuous surrender or nothing. Just becoming life itself is the only possibility on this path. That means complete release of the drama of self in any form. The pursuit of all experience, regardless of how base and depraved or refined and transcendent, is also part of the drama of self. When there is no drama, then no war is won, no victory is had. There is just life. Life in all its glory, as Glory—every ordinary, simple moment and corner of it. When progression along this path appears to one as a big deal, either that it is going so badly or going so well, it is just impurities getting kicked up—impurities that we hope will fall by the way as a natural process of the Work. The feeling that one is doing anything, or that the results one is getting are good or bad, is just the wave that occurs in the psyche as what is personal is purged from one's consciousness on the way to becoming simple and ordinary, yet radiant in life.

&

It's a fallacy that anyone can choose "what is." This is like asking someone to eat himself. It's impossible. Realizing "what is" is not a choice or an action. It is what finally occurs when one reaches the real dead end of choosing what *isn't* over and over and over again. Then, one day, "what is" chooses us. Not the other way around. This may sound like semantics, but the mood is completely different. It is the difference between a self-help method or improvement course through which we, at base, are still trying to change ourselves, and surrender to the Divine, which cannot be done by anyone. It can only be done to us. Helplessness, hopelessness, longing—yes. But choice? No. That puts the ball too much in our own court, which is the only thing we're suffering from in the first place: the belief that we can act, that we can do something. Any effort we make whatsoever, no matter how good it sounds, is still coming from exactly the same place. Until it's not. And when it's not, we will know it without a doubt.

જી

The Work is all about becoming able to rest in Nothingness, craving Nothingness, and turning to Nothingness in all circumstances, situations, and relationships. The fact is, ego wants to feel something, experience something. Those feelings, sensations, and experiences are the very basis of its ability to self-reference, because in any experience there seems to be "one" who is experiencing. As we adhere more and more to the all-encompassing Reality and Truth of the Infinite, we are turning our awareness to the static quality of the universe in such a way that many of the things we used to relate to as an "experience" fade so much into the background that we barely notice them anymore, even though they are still occurring. So the pleasantries, comforts, or discomforts we once reacted to so passionately begin to slide by with little notice, care, or concern, since the concern, over time, turns to the Context of the Absolute, which transcends experience.

The lengths to which ego will go to avoid this Nothingness as a resting place and predominant residence for consciousness can be nothing short of all-out warfare, where no means is considered outside the bounds of fair play, including bringing great harm to others or oneself. The way to cook a frog is a relevant analogy. A frog thrown directly into boiling water will jump right out, but one put in cold water that is slowly heated will allow itself to be boiled into a meal. This work is best done very slowly, gradually, and thoroughly. Too speedy or premature efforts can cause backlashes and side effects that can provoke ego to drastic measures and cause significant damage to oneself or one's relationships.

A two-frame cartoon shows three men who have just fallen into a black hole of nothingness and are plummeting into a bottomless abyss. They're screaming and look terror stricken, clawing for any kind of hold in this emptiness. In the second frame, the same men are still falling into the same blackness, but now one of them is reading a book, the second is filing his nails, and the third is eating a sandwich. After a while we're able to function in an ordinary way even in the face of Nothingness, but this is not the initial response.

God is none other than this Nothingness. The closer we come to Him, the closer we are to having to face this great unknown and the terror that will arise in response. We can dance around the edges as long as we want, but once we enter completely into His company, the chamber of His Heart, we must face Reality, the static Truth of the Universe, the yawning abyss of Creation. This is death. Exactly and none other than death. So how can this be done? It must be clear that ego never can and never will choose such a thing. One way to trick ego is to use the cooking-a-frog technique. Make the work and progress so incremental that it hardly registers the dissolution of itself. But still, there is that final moment. And there is no way that ego is not going to notice in that final moment, no matter what the approach. This is the greatest miracle in the universe; the miracle in which ego willingly allows itself to expire to allow the possibility of God in its place.

≥≥

Nondualism as it is constantly bantered about as a phrase is actually good-feelingism. Nondualism does not exist. As a concept it can only shadow dualism; therefore, since it is not complete unto itself, it remains dualism. In unity consciousness there is no one to experience nondualism. It is not an experience. It just is.

Unity consciousness is not there to recognize either the separation of things or the unity of things. It doesn't sigh as it observes that things are unified and go, "Ah, nondualism."

≥≥

Relationship happens when God is central and one actually comes to feel that one *is* the thing or person that one is relating to. But this is actually not relationship because then one is not "relating" to anything outside of, or other than, oneself. The very definition of relationship implies some sort of connecting up of two things. All the psychotherapeutic systems that claim to teach people how to be "in relationship" will sooner or later fail for anyone who uses them with any degree of self-honesty and self-observation, because in spite of the mental and emotional gymnastics they've been taught, such a person will recognize that they are still "relating" from a position of separation.

Relationship, in fact, never happens. It can't happen. Only God can happen, and when God happens, it is not that everything gets joined or becomes related, it's that the idea of there being two vanishes, and so the thought, idea, or effort to "join" things together or connect them up simply becomes obsolete. Of course, for this to happen one must take refuge in God. Through this refuge the identification with the body/mind is vacated, expanded upon infinitely, completely released. This is the way to the discovery of Oneness. The very effort to "create relationship" is absurd from a conscious position. The one trying to create relationship cannot be related, because true relatedness springs from complete surrender, complete relaxation.

ॐ

So much of modern day spirituality is nothing more than the activity of denial, the attempt to avoid what is Real based on the conditioning to reject parts of our psychophysical makeup. All the things we have been trained to believe are "bad," "wrong," and "shouldn't be" we reject and cover up with a "spirituality" which denies and focuses on an exclusive field of attention. This is never and cannot be God.

The world of form is undeniable, nor should it be denied. The heart of the spiritual process is not to deny, avoid, take away, or limit form, but to add to it, expand around it, embrace it; to know what it is that includes form, not that which rejects or is other than form. To rest eternally in this formlessness that includes form but is not limited to or bound by form is to know God. Who we are includes our body and mind but is not our body and mind. Spirituality is always inclusive, not exclusive. It must be inclusive because it is Everything.

ॐ

It's all coming apart at the seems. The way everything has always seemed to be is disintegrating, unwinding, not holding water anymore. To come apart at the seems is to have everything that seems to be unravel, so that attitudes, beliefs, opinions and judgments no longer have any binding power or ability to make "sense" of the universe. And when one can no longer make sense of the universe, then and only then does it appear for the first time as it is. The paradox is that it is only seeing things as they are which has the power to unravel what seems to be. A glimpse, through grace, of "what is," beyond and prior to mind, creates responsibility for the practitioner to build upon the momentum of this glimpse, through surrender and practice; to further his or her awareness of the futility of "making sense" of the universe.

In the Land of Oz the scarecrow was attacked by flying monkeys who took him apart, dismembered him; a leg over there, an arm over here. Spiritual work is about entering the Land of Is. In the Land of Is we get taken apart by the playful monkeys of God. Allowing this to happen is how a straw man becomes a Real man.

இ

Self-acceptance is such a radical thing. When practiced fully it cannot be separated from the ultimate necessity to accept Everything. Self-acceptance is nothing more or less than the acceptance of Everything as it is. But the idea has been so watered down by popular therapy and self-help methods that its effectiveness has been drowned by the mediocrity of those applying it. Self-acceptance in these circles is the directive to not look too deeply, to not enquire to the point of discomfort, typified by such advice as, "Give yourself a break. You deserve it."

Ruthless self-honesty is the only possibility. To be completely and fully honest, deeply curious, obsessively hungry for what is True and then unapologetic about exactly what one is is the only way to become available to the storm of Love that grace brings.

≥•

We are born into this world as millionaires. The human vehicle as a child is so fluently and naturally aligned to the energy of the entire Universe that we have it all in the palm of our hand. For most people, everything after that is a process of losing this fortune, penny by penny, until one day we die a pauper. What a grim view. But that is increasingly the process of growing old in the modern world without the benefit of any education about, appreciation for, or exposure to living a life in God.

≥•

Who we truly are is to the body/mind what the beach is to the grain of sand. The grain of sand is certainly part of what makes up the beach, but if that grain of sand gets blown away, the beach remains. The grain is relevant to the beach, but not essential to the beach. Such is the truth of ego.

≥•

If this is it, then the whole path is a complete and utter joke! What a con! To work so hard for so long to wind up with nothing but what one had all along, just exactly "what is" and what always was, but with the very simple, ordinary, and obvious Truth that there is no one associated with this. It is utterly simple. Nothing special. If there is no one there to live the life of the human, there is only the Divine left to live it, and what the Divine does with such a life may look completely ordinary or very extraordinary, but the life is then no longer being managed by the agenda of the illusory body, since the body has ceased to be in exclusive control. Then God can spontaneously animate the life of the one who is "not there,"—not trying to make life look like anything at all, with no investment or resistance to whatever arises.

&

Here is this man who has always hoped to come out a shining hero on the other side of the phone booth of transformation. What a great joke! This condition has no audience and never will. Now, for a performer, attention hound, and exhibitionist like this man, that's a bit of a bummer. But for God, it is a very wonderful and juicy sting—a grand affair in the lila of it all—to watch one who wanted attention most of all be totally and utterly foiled in the possibility of gaining recognition for the only thing worth being recognized for. Joy to the Lord; may He be well amused. He shall have many days of fine humor while witnessing this body/mind try to twist this phenomenon into something for itself, some way to capitalize on this bizarre condition.

&

There is no way anyone can articulate what is essentially transcendental in language, and even if they could, it would not, could not, be received for what it is by anyone to whom the experience would be worth communicating; that is, who isn't already experiencing the same thing. People just hear what they are capable of hearing, which is, at worst, a reduction of the communication to what they are committed to proving at the survival level or, at best, a pigeonholing of what is being described into a box that they already have a reference for, which, even if it's the best box they've got, still destroys the possibility of receiving the essence of the communication. Furthermore, any recognition that is given by anyone to another who attempts to make such a communication is not founded on a perception of what is truly happening for the communicator, but only of what someone else imagines, projects or assumes is happening as prompted by their observation of the visible phenomena and their assumptions and interpretations about what such phenomena signify.

❧

It could be safely asserted that most "spiritual" seekers who embark on the path have, as their unconscious motivation, the aim of finally becoming important, getting acknowledgment, becoming loved, et cetera. When success on the path renders one completely unimportant, unrecognizable, unacknowledged, unrewarded, unknown, not understood, invisible, and nothing more than a pawn in service to the desperate and tangled attempts of everyone else's quest for importance and acknowledgment and love, then God's preposterously delicious sense and style of humor is revealed. Here's to it!

❧

The upshot of all our karma is that we are bound to shadow the activity of a human body/mind. Since we are connected to all its activity, it is understandable that we take it and its manifestations as us. There is ordinarily no break, no gap in which we get a reference for the possibility that all of this activity has nothing to do with us at all. The difference occurs when, through a great deal of passionate self-observation and the eventual intervention of grace, we glimpse through a crack that we only perfectly follow this activity of the body/mind, but remain absolutely distinct from it at the same time. The body/mind and consciousness are like the two rails that parallel each other to carry a train. These two elements work together, are both necessary, but they never intersect and are always exactingly apart.

※

A World War II veteran pilot was being interviewed on a documentary program about the history of the use of airplanes in battle. He said, "War is ninety-nine percent boredom and one percent terror." This is also a fitting description of the spiritual path.

※

To cut the root of anger we must simply see it exactly as it is. Not make it into anything more or less than what it is, not take ownership or have it be "me" that is getting angry. When Everything is God, even anger, it is just energy, and when it is seen this way there is a relaxation that doesn't allow the anger to harm. Anger is like water contracted as ice. You couldn't hurt anyone with a handful of water, but throwing an ice-hard snowball at someone has a different impact. Surrender is the key. Feeling, remaining present, accepting what arises without judgment.

But even if we hear this kind of rhetoric over and over it may make no difference. We may still do the same old thing in relationship to our anger. It is not a shift of mentality. Intellect cannot carry "just this." We have to hop on God's back, at least for a time, to get from here to there. The old phrase, "You can't get there from here," is relevant, except in spiritual work there is the additional proviso, ". . . except on God's back." Only God's Influence can help us with this. Without His Influence, what hope is there for all our words, thoughts, even the Teaching? The Teaching without the living Reality of God is a dead and empty affair, a bullet without gunpowder; no explosive for delivery, a blank.

Transformation is the difference between thinking we have to "do something" with our thoughts, feelings, and urges and just seeing them all as an expression of God and letting them be without necessarily having to express them. Transformation involves trusting that if expression is appropriate that expression will arise from the context of seeing it all as God, and if God chooses to express Himself in any way at any given moment, so be it. This trust extends to all negativity. Negativity seen as God is never chosen by God to be expressed—and when it is, it is no longer negative, but creative and serving.

❧

Due to our upbringing and conditioning, many thoughts which we judge or label as "unpure" cross our minds in any given period. The Masters of many spiritual traditions talk about the absolute necessity for a completely pure mind and how important it is to become completely free of vanity, greed, anger, shame, and other negative states. If we adopt this advice mechanically and prop up the old mind, using these statements to solidify this wall where

God is on one side and the parts of us which are greedy, lustful, angry, et cetera, are seen as "not God," we've handicapped ourselves on the path.

In truth, all these energies in us are also God, no better or worse than other energies, thoughts, or feelings. To become aware of this and practice the assertion of it can unite us not only with all of "ourselves," but with everyone and Everything. When the judgment about certain energies, manifestations, and states within ourselves is lifted and we are willing to stand in noncritical observation of ourselves as we are, a perspective arrives that frees up our energy to transcend the "impure" or lower forms of energy and thoughts. This is key to the process—this acceptance and inclusion of all our parts. It is the basis of tantric practice. Tantra is like doing aikido with God and all of His manifestations. Not fighting with "what is," but redirecting it.

ॐ

What we become once the light of God is allowed to penetrate us is determined by a combination of the Divine and the personal. Without God, the personal aspects of an individual can do only one thing: suck. They want to survive and can only survive when fed by external sources. So they prey on manifest reality, manipulating it with gravitational forces that are psychologically neurotic and self-preserving. In this way, these personal aspects capture food in their little mouths and swallow it, digesting it into the black hole of themselves. Then, with hardly a pause, they insatiably turn to plunder the outer world for more.

When "what is" is realized internally, however, the Glory of the Divine radiates from the heart. Shining outward, pure and undifferentiated, it reaches these same personal traits and aspects and is refracted in a unique way. The personal refraction of the light of God from within is the manifest expression of God and God's love in human form.

We are not to do away with the personal, the individual, in spiritual work. We are simply presented with the Work of radiating God outwardly through what is personal so that we become an expression of the Divine instead of stealing "what is" for our personal bottomless hole, which can do nothing but greedily devour God's creation in perpetuation of itself.

இ

How can we create the kind of necessity that allows us to stop being transfixed by, trapped in, and stuck with our self-obsessive, self-referenced, and self-concerned perspective of "the Work"? Most of the "spiritual" considerations, reflections, discussions, and ideas that are floating around nowadays go absolutely nowhere, and never will go anywhere. Take the example of a person who is in a room with a door which is barricaded with furniture piled up against it, put there by the person himself. We are like the person who spends forever asking questions like, "I wonder what my motivation is for putting all that furniture there? Why do I hate myself so much that I would want to block myself in here like this? What is the nature of the reality that is outside of that door?" But if by chance an electrical fire were to start in that room, you can be sure that we would stop asking these questions immediately and begin instead to act on clearing the furniture away from the door. We must have great necessity for the Work to which we say we are dedicated. God Himself can provide such a necessity. God is outside, on the other side of the door. If we glimpse Him through the window and work to keep our attention on Him, then we will find ourselves one day clearing away the furniture without even being aware that we are doing so, since our attention is then irresistibly drawn to the elegance, grace, intelligence, sanity, and benediction of God. Whatever needs to happen then to attain access to what we have developed necessity for gets handled without discussion, debate, or deliberation.

ॐ

Fish need oxygen to survive. They breathe it, but not like humans do. Fish are built to get oxygen by extracting it from a more complex substance; water, of course. Humans have the ability to breathe in air and use the oxygen present in the atmosphere more directly. But when it comes to knowing God, we are more like fish. We have to jump into the substance of life, and if we breathe deeply into that, life will filter over our souls and God will become available to us, but only through an embrace of the whole solution in which He is suspended. Our bodies are like a fish's gills. We must inhale all of Life and trust the intelligence of the design to deliver to us the breath of the Divine.

ॐ

You don't have to look too deeply to see how ridiculous all human striving is. It is all based on the false assumption that "I can win." There is absolutely nothing one can do to win. We will, without doubt, inherent in the nature of humanness, lose at the game we are trying so desperately to win; the game we hope will allow us to survive in eternal human comfort and happiness, or to survive eternally in any condition, for that matter. In any hope or belief that we can help ourselves, save ourselves, find an alternative at the last minute, or escape our predicament in any way, there is no possibility.

ஜ

It all boils down to just faith. All that is required is the faith that God will win in the end; the faith that God has already won, that it is all already perfect, the way of God. The instant a moment has passed which the mind has labeled "not God," there is nothing to do but to reset one's sights on His perfection and surrender to the Truth of this with all of one's heart.

There are two immense and profound joys in life. The first is that of resting in the perfection of God in each moment. The second occurs in the instant that, realizing we've forgotten the first joy, we abandon such distraction then and there without a thought and return again to the glory of His perfection. Since there are only two possible states in which we can find ourselves—remembrance of God and the forgetfulness which God has produced as an invitation to remember —this news is cause for nothing but joy.

ஜ

# THE NATURE OF MIND

Just behind the appearance of things is a raging present moment, unfathomably dynamic, breathtakingly new, altogether alive. If we want this, we must look for it in every instant that the mind already thinks it knows what is going on, who we are, and what anything is.

Our attention must shift from the appearance of things to the unknown and unknowable space between the particles of all that we believe we see and know. To the space that appearances cannot touch. There is, in fact, an infinitely yawning gap between each particle of matter, a universal womb from which streams the endless wonder of creation, and of the unknown.

Once we learn to look into creation this way, we will be willing to leave the appearance of things completely alone, not trying to control or influence superficial appearances as if how they manifested had anything to do with our essential well-being and happiness. Whatever appears then, we will know the knack of journeying between the fragments of any perception to that which is beyond all manifestation. We will cut through what seems to be true to the mind and pierce ordinary reality like an arrow, quickening to the heart of God.

Be in love without a lover. Feel the thrill of victory without winning a thing. Take up residence in a magnificent palace without moving. Gather all the facts and draw no conclusions. This generosity alone, extended toward the Truth which is Lord, will cause that One to seek us even more passionately than we are seeking Him.

꩜

This ego thing, the idea of being someone who is separate, is worse than just an idea. It's a bad idea. It's an unexamined, illogical, and blind idea. Spirituality is not just mystical. It's also logical. Even on the grossest level, taking into consideration what any of us can perceive through our senses, disregarding all the subtle realities of energy exchange, there are real, tangible substances that go in and out of our body—air, food, water, to begin with—that sustain us, without which we would literally be nothing as a body. Then, on a slightly more subtle level, there are impressions—the touch or words of another, other ideas, the warmth of the sun—which affect us, give us energy, passion, move us forward, support us, or block us. How can we nurture the illusion of separation in the face of such facts? Our determined insistence that our bodies are "ours" and everything else is "not ours" is insane. But when everyone agrees to exist under the guise of the same illusions, then there is no discussion, examination, or notice of them since there is no conflict about them. Everyone agrees. When we begin to question the belief systems the world has unanimously agreed to abide by, there are bound to be a few shocks. The discrepancy between how one has been conditioned to live, when observed alongside the unadorned Truth, can be startling, unnerving, and even maddening.

ൟ

Everyone is trying to make a shift to this thing called the "awakened" or "enlightened" perspective. It's ridiculous. Take the phrase, "I have to shift my perspective." Notice that the focus falls on the words "shift" and "perspective," as if the key to the whole ball game were located there, in "shifting perspective." We think, "Ah, yes. How I would like a new perspective," when actually our sense of "I" is the only thing worth examining and working with in the consideration.

What we're truly after is perspective which has no registered owner. Then perspective is just perspective and we cannot be imprisoned in identification with it. Perspective is always just perspective. Any perspective is just perspective. No more. A shift in perspective is just trading in our Dodge for a Plymouth. We're still stuck with a domestic auto.

❧

"Mind" is the only "problem" or obstacle to God realization. There is, in reality, no separation, no problem. It is only in mind that a dilemma exists. The purpose of practice is for one thing: to develop mastery over and discipline the mind. Mind must be made strong, a strong servant. That strength will feed ego, and ego must become strong in very specific ways so that it can eventually feed on itself. This is what transformation is—a strong ego eating itself and creating Nothing where it used to be. That is the symbolism of the snake eating itself by the tail. The practice of right thinking, right use of mind, or Jnana Yoga is only a process of training the mind to know and submit to a boss who is not the mind. All such practice boils down to that: training and taming the mind.

❧

"I" is only a collection of wrong ideas that we get from someone else, the individual components of which cling to each other and form a wad. Like old chewing gum that is left on the ground, if we are unlucky enough to step on it, it gets stuck on the bottom of our soul. "I" is just that extraneous to who we really are, just that degree of distraction, and even harder to get off.

❧

Flying home on a plane, drifting far, far above passing farmland and stretched out highways, even the mountains look manageable. But suddenly the mind is in the primitive grip of the densest thought a human can have. The thought is, "I could die right now." The reality of the impending, inevitable, if not immediate, death of self is magnetized into awareness by the circumstance of flying; hanging in mid-air over cloud in a piece of speeding metal that weighs an untold number of tons.

I try to stay with the feeling—to let it all the way in—that the current fear is appropriate, not necessarily because death is going to happen in this circumstance, but because the self will eventually, without a doubt, in some circumstance, DIE. But the mind just won't go there, and it skates out from beneath the pressure of my attention like mercury. The spiritually educated part of the mind tries to argue with it. "You're fooling yourself, death is certain." But it is no use. It is arguing with the Time Warner corporation of the mind. There are simply too many expressions of the entity's control, dominance, and vested interests to make any headway with it straight on. There must be more clever means. Thankfully, there are back doors, and You are the Master of them. You teach us these ways to get in and train us to be good thieves. You who teach us the art of stealing back our own souls would never recommend walking straight into the front office and announcing our intentions. The way of the sly man is what You teach.

Suddenly, looking down at the ground again, You intervene and pierce what the mind has done. In convincing itself that there is nothing holding the airplane up in this thin air, it has created fear for itself out of just that: thin air. The truth is, air is just as real, as tangible, and as solid as anything else. It simply cannot be seen by the eyes, and so the fear arises. The same is so with grace. The truth is, the universe rides on invisible-to-the-eyes grace, like the airplane on the transparent air. If we look at "what is," come out of denial about "what is," then what it is that supports that which is becomes apparent and obvious.

Admit that the plane is flying and you will see the air. Admit what you are as a human being and you will see and know the reality of grace.

≥≥

Over time, meditation will clearly and steadily provide the greatest revelation: that everything one has been transfixed and imprisoned by, that all concern with matter, with everything one calls oneself, with the apparent existence of life itself, is simply an illusion—an appearance created by having one's attention limited to one very thin slice of reality.

In practicing meditation, there is an energy that becomes more and more available to our direct experience. We'll use the word "experience" only because we do not have a better word to describe it. It is the condition of there being only One all pervasive and completely unformed and undifferentiated energy or life force that is radiating through, past, into, beyond, around, and within Everything. Acknowledgment of or the turning of full attention to this energy results in a perspective from which nothing is, nothing can be, nothing comes into matter. Matter is the phenomenon of thinking, of mind limiting its attention to a very small facet or a part of Infinity.

The process of doing spiritual practice is what helps the body/mind to host a range of sensations which are not overwhelming to the possibility of feeling energy at a very subtle and refined level. God energy is infinitely more subtle than thought, feelings, emotions, or physical sensations. If all of these sensing forms are constantly in turmoil and producing high levels of stimulation, it is much more difficult—maybe impossible—to even glimpse, but certainly to sustain, an awareness of these subtler layers of energy and perception. So abusing the body, living in chaos, distress, confusion, having incomplete projects, relationships, and plans all shroud finer senses of energy with a distracting and overriding tension.

When one's attention is on Nothing, then nothing matters. That is, nothing can become imprisoned in matter if one's attention is on nothing. It is impossible to have one's attention on nothing and feel that things matter. These are exact opposites.

&

The perceived separateness of objects and manifestations in place and time is supported by the way we are trained to think about things and the conditioning that has been linked to what is seen by the eyes. For instance, when the eyes see a person begging on the street the vision may be accompanied by the conditioned perception that such a person is poor, dirty, unintelligent, pitiful, sad, irresponsible, needy, and possibly dangerous. Because this conditioned interpretation includes the judgment that all those things are "bad," we separate ourselves internally and energetically from the beggar. To see with or act based upon clear vision is to have an entirely different layer of information available to us and allows for the possibility of acting and being from a non-separative, compassionate, and enlightened perspective—"enlightened" meaning without the ability to be fooled by appearances. All appearances are formed by the conditioned mind that boxes up the world into packages and automatically tags the things it "sees" through the eyes with conditioned responses.

At a true feeling level of present awareness, a level from which we see with the Heart, our "body" loses its distinct edges, "what is" towers wondrously over our preconceptions and assumptions, and all the "tags" wither up and vanish into a mystery that is beyond description.

≥•

It is essential and necessary to have an intentional and formal relationship to spiritual practice, companionship, and guidance—but along with that territory comes a lot of ideas and concepts that we take as the path or the goal itself, and until everything that we come to "know" about this Work gets absolutely undermined and challenged to the point of the complete devastation of our belief system, there is no possibility for transformation.

Grace will absolutely not tolerate any idea about what it is, how it comes, or what form it should or might take. It is only in absolute surrender of any idea about it whatsoever that grace can offer what it has. Never before such surrender. It will not waste itself on any preconceived notions of what it truly means to be Alive. Grace is uncompromising in the conditions it demands from its guest. Unconditional faith and devotion are the demand. "No idea" is the admission fee.

≥•

It is the refined ego that must be guarded against with due vigilance; feared and respected as the formidable opponent that it is. Since a refined ego is often the exact trait which we with spiritual ambition are endowed, and usually continue to refine rather than diminish on the path, as we work it is easier for us to get caught in the web of deceit that ego spins, not harder. As we develop immunity to ego's ploys and attempts to snare us into allegiance to its aims, it immediately mutates and runs ahead along the path to fashion another pit we have not yet seen and may fall into. It is not that we have to pass ego once and consider the battle done. We must pass it many, many times. Every day, moment to moment, over and over. Thus the necessity of the guidance of a wisdom which knows all the tricks already.

ॐ

Exactly what we experience, and precisely the very "experience" we are currently immersed in, is "what is" in this moment. And "what is" is exactly what it is supposed to be, perfectly and without any deviation from Divine will. The instant this tweaks in us, our entire relationship to the moment shifts, without the content of the moment shifting itself at all. The mind is able to continuously forge layers of ignorance that it can and will paste over even the most profound experiences, rendering them equally or more of a contributor to ignorance and illusion than even ordinary experiences.

All mental, physical, or spiritual phenomena, the sense of higher consciousness states, and all perceived progress toward knowing God experientially is just the by-product of what mind does when it is confronted by and then interprets the Divine. Without mind there would be no experience at all. No special states. No phenomena. Just life. And all of life would be seen to be the same Presence with no need for any special or "extraordinary" states occurring to support, justify, or prove the existence of the Divine or to strive to attain it.

Does acting the will of God in one's life exactly correspond to the conscious awareness that everything one does, thinks, says, and feels *is* the will of God without fail, with no possibility of it being otherwise?

ᥲ

Sentimentality is only a re-creation of our past. When we bring our past to the present, the present loses the luminous edge that it needs to penetrate human consciousness and create Life within a human being. An inner structure in a practitioner is only built up over the repeated gathering or collection of present moments, real moments, untainted by the past. An inner structure is necessary to be able to hold the kind of energy we need for our transformation.

Sentimentality destroys the food which, if it were processed in a different way, could form the foundation of this inner structure.

Taking in life "as it is" is like eating whole foods. Whole foods stimulate simultaneous digestion processes in the body that need to work all at the same time in order to absorb energy in a way that balances and harmonizes the human machine. Receiving a wide range of impressions through our senses in any given moment, as they are, is necessary in the same way at a different level of food. Impression food that is not taken as whole food—that is, impressions that are filtered through conditionings, belief systems, obsessions/compulsions or sentimentality— are pre-digested and broken down so their complexity and sophistication does not reach consciousness, and consciousness is deprived of the opportunity to rise to the occasion of digesting a complex quality of food.

This is how we weaken consciousness and how its maturation can be effectively retarded or altogether undermined. Consciousness requires an opportunity to do the work of digesting the complex and sophisticated structures of Reality. Without this work to do, it atrophies; just like a colon that never gets roughage, that only eats predigested food, can become weak or dis-eased. The stark nature of

Reality, as it is, not as it fits into our pre-conceived notions of what it is, so challenges the mind and consciousness that it calls consciousness to work at an entirely different level, a level beyond the mechanical and survival faculties housed within it. There are distinct parts of the mind, and the part that is responsible for ensuring our physical survival is a very small part of its actual potential, although practically the only part which is developed in us. The parts of our minds which are designed to be activated after survival is ensured and a healthy ego has been established are those parts which can lead us into profound creativity and a relationship to revelation, intuition, and spirit; but this can only occur when the appropriate training is present for that mind.

The technology for the kind of training and practice required to activate these higher functions in the mind is all but lost and nonexistent in North American culture. We must make a specific effort and undertake a specific training to activate this capacity within ourselves. Learning how to take in whole impression food that is not processed and butchered in the factory of the mechanical mind is essential to challenge consciousness directly in such a way that it begins to respond to the infinite mystery of Reality and becomes ultimately able to handle the cognition of Reality directly in all its complexity, paradox, flux, and contradiction. This is what meditation as a practice is for: to eliminate the middleman, conditioned mind, who is raking in huge profits and siphoning off enormous amounts of energy, and let Reality deal directly with the cognizing part of the mind. This direct contact between Reality and consciousness is the only way to build the strength and energy we need to go the distance on this path.

ॐ

Denial is the intellectual posture that something should not exist when it actually *does* exist. The intellect creates an argument that something does not exist with strategic ignorance and other intellectual and psychological resources rather than face the feelings that arise in the acknowledgment of "what is."

We need to go precisely where we have been profoundly trained not to go; to a level of energetic openness and expansion where we are unbuffered, immensely vulnerable, unprotected, and surrendered to Everything that is. We did exist in such a condition once as an infant, but there was not at that time a mature enough structure in place to sustain full feeling and simultaneously digest some of the more toxic impressions which are routinely delivered to newborns and young children in this modern culture. Such a structure must be built by the spiritual practitioner and is literally a framework or body of distinctions that is creative, intelligent, and reflective of the complexity and intelligence of the universe—of "what is."

The value of being able to make more and more refined distinctions is so that we don't have to throw the baby out with the bath water. Separating the wheat from the chaff can only be accomplished with the right tool. If you don't have the right tool, the only option is to reject the whole crop that life and humanness is. The more refined one's practice becomes, the more refined the tools or distinctions must become to support a higher level of work, which must embrace an infinite number of complexities, paradoxes, and contradictions.

❧

Impression food is for the purpose of letting the soul gather enough impressions through the senses to realize full Reality. There is a cross-referencing that goes on through which the soul, filtering a wide range of impressions, finally realizes the one thread which is common to them all: the thread of Reality. This realization requires the processing of a great number of impressions which, at first, form a belief system and fixed notions about the way the world is. But if impression food continues to be digested without survival needs creating a strong attachment to any particular interpretation of them, the impressions will eventually cancel each other out until the all-abiding unknowableness of Everything is revealed through the process.

But most people stop gathering fresh impressions long before this happens. It requires only a small amount of contamination by any given culture's way of interpreting Reality to start a landslide of dissociation from what is True. After initial indoctrination into their culture's slant on the world, most people gather impressions that, instead of being introduced into an internal sanctuary where their innocence and purity are protected, are immediately fertilized with unconscious conditionings—mechanical and artificial associations which start to grow like weeds in the garden of Eden, the garden of "what is." Then, when further impressions come along, those impressions are modified by the mind to fit with the conditionings that have been formed on the basis of the previous or early life impressions. In this way the cultural, family, religious, parental, and societal belief system that is set in place at the beginning of an individual's life is not only protected, but is vehemently defended by those very people who suffer from the prisons of these modified and sterilized versions of reality.

૨૭

We think the world is full of things. It is not. To completely be with all perceivable things is to know the Universe as utterly empty. The only thing that can occupy space is mind. "What is" has no weight, no size, and is no burden whatsoever. Even the grossest layer of existence is actually nothing and is definitely not a problem or obstacle. Only mind and its interpretations are obstacles to Infinity, to God, to spirituality; not anything that is.

෨

Today, while reading a book to the children, there came the sense that laying there reading them the book was absolutely no more nor less an "experience" of God than all the blissed-out states that occur in meditation. The mind still keeps two categories of experience: God and not God. If exactly whatever it is that is experienced is left to be what it is, and only what it is, then all experience is God; and if all experience is God, then that's the end of experience. An experience must begin and end. God does not begin and end. Which is why all our efforts to "experience" God will always and forever fail.

෨

It is misleading to say that our work is about the ability to perceive another reality, about having eyes to see something that we do not currently see. It is closer to the truth to say that our work is about *not looking* at something to which we are currently and exclusively riveted. When our attention is freed from what we are habitually focused on and constantly holding in our vision, the simple Truth becomes our vision. Reality appears when our vision is whole, open, unbiased, and free; not when we are preoccupied with seeing something in particular, as we continue to be even in the "spiritual" search. Any type of search or desire results in a limited seeing, a fragmented perception of "what is." When we are looking for something in particular—a result, a goal, or a realization—a grasp of what is

True is impeded by a blockade of conditioning, by a wall of beliefs and preconceptions. We all come to the spiritual path looking to prove something, looking for an opportunity to justify our obsession with the type of vision we have always been practicing. The discovery of this obsession in ourselves is crucial to our progress on the path, especially with respect to how it is manifesting in our own spiritual work; for example, we've always been ambitious and now that ambition is aimed at gaining the prize of "awakening" or "enlightenment."

As the preoccupation that has been conditioned into us is relaxed, bit by bit, there comes a time when the whole balance of power gets flipped over. Then, instead of there being glimpses of Truth that make their way somehow into our context of separation, there are periods of ego identification that arise from time to time in the Context of Truth. This happens not so much from looking for or seeking God or the Divine as it does from looking directly at our sense of separation itself, which results, over time, in our awareness piercing that illusion.

So our work is not about looking for, but about looking at. This shifts us from the unreal to the Real. We can easily spend decades looking *for* our fantasy. We can't spend any amount of time looking at a fantasy because, of course, it doesn't exist. If we try to look at it, we will very quickly discover that it doesn't exist. If we try to look for it, we may not discover that for a long, long time. We will only convince ourselves that we have not looked in the right places, or in the right manner, and the search will go on.

❧

Eventually, as the disappearance of "oneself" becomes more and more allowable, more routine in meditation, we simply have to sit down and close our eyes to drop in. Just the words "let go," or "surrender," can produce the unraveling of identification that leads us quickly to the Source, to vulnerability, to Divine Influence. But there is clearly a distinction which has something to do with the difference between deep meditation and annihilation. In deep meditation moments may arise when annihilation sweeps just by us, grazes us, but does not strike us, and we get a reminder of what kind of attachment to "ourselves" remains. In such instances, the terror arises automatically, and something in us tenses and cannot say, in that moment, that it is ready to die. Of course it never will. So it is a curious thing to see in this process of surrender how God will ultimately and finally take over completely when our mind still holds on to some sense of self. There is no possibility of its letting go of its own accord. We can only watch and wait and long and pray.

❧

Trying to get recognition and attention from others for our personal security is such a pitiful and mediocre substitute for the Attention of the Divine. We are already and always the object of His complete Attention. Unless we turn inward we shall never know this and instead will look outward for something which can never be gained from an outwardly seeking perspective.

"I" is only an idea—a bunch of repeated ideas—the repetition of beliefs that create the illusion of separation. But through meditation, the Great Shift can occur. We discover that, in fact, there is no boundary. The morning-breaking birdsong, the cows mooing, the church bells echoing in space, the roosters crowing. God is Everything! To exist as All is the only life. Then everything of which we have been trying to rid ourselves can be accepted. All of it. Mind, emotion, habit. In knowing All, our standard identification with what we take as "us" is pulled so thin that we can see right through the identification to the Truth of there being no one truly associated with all these things. There are just "those things." Just "what is." Just all this phenomena arising everywhere all the time. Ego is simply the habit of singling out various phenomena and identifying with them, a completely self-perpetuating habit that in Reality simply does not exist. In Reality there are simply "those things" without anyone to be in relationship to them. This is the Truth. This Truth and the direct perception of it is the source of Love. The very essence of Love. There is no one "loving" at that point. There is just what is called the "prior condition," and that condition is Love.

ૐ

To be undistractible does not mean that we are so focused on one particular thing that our awareness is riveted to that thing to the exclusion of all else. To be undistractible is to already have Everything in our attention. If this is so, there is nothing that can surprise us, blindside us, take us over, and cause us to lose attention to the Whole. Distraction occurs when awareness narrows to the extent that it forgets the Whole. It is no great feat to manage to get ourselves more concerned with one thing over another. That is just the petty tyranny of ordinary mind.

ૐ

Vision always sees things without separation. What vision sees is one scene. It is all One. It is only mind that creates boundaries and divisions between things, butchering them up to sell off in the mind's meat market: a bone for this "I", a bone for that "I". Meditation is essential; so crucial to the spiritual process. It is the way to pierce the illusion of separation. If practiced consistently, it is reliable and it works. But before meditation can help to pierce the illusion, we have to come out of denial about illusion. It's not profitable to our Work to call our suffering "just an illusion" to lessen the discomfort of our circumstance, since that only imprisons us longer in the illusion itself. The illusion vanishes only when we look right at it, feel the full extent of it. It is the suffering produced by living the lie that provides the possibility for us to go beyond the lie. The illusion is sustained by the avoidance of full feeling.

❧

To be human and deny the existence of God because He cannot be understood by the intellect is like being a cellular biologist who denies the existence of elephants because they won't fit under his microscope.

❧

Certain kinds of thoughts—for example, internally considered aggression—can spill over into the creation of what could be called karma. That is, they accumulate a force which penetrates and leaves a residue in the unconscious, which at some point must come back out the very door through which the thoughts were driven in. When they come back out, they must come out through consciousness. This means that at some point the very same thoughts will appear again on the surface of the mind. When that occurs, there are two possibilities. One is to react to them, take action on them, reinforce and deepen them, which drives them back into unconsciousness even more strongly and intensifies the vicious circle. The second option is, through this understanding of what is happening, to simply observe these thoughts and sensations and watch them arise and then subside of their own accord, which accomplishes their release, or at least weakening, from the complex of the body/mind. This second response must go on for a long, long time before we begin to experience the lightening or burning off of reactive tendencies we have been feeding all our lives or, for all we know, even many lives.

ə.

In meditation one may find oneself skating on the surface of thoughts and sensations, with mind wandering. If surrender is practiced in the face of what would otherwise descend into an obsession with what "isn't happening" or isn't "right" about the meditation—with the shallowness of the meditation—a moment arises when a crack is left for the Influence to get in and start to work its magic. Once in, it spreads through ordinary thought and begins to devour whatever it finds as food for the unknown. Suddenly sensations, sounds, thoughts all begin to lead to the deep well of emptiness that leads to more surrender; to the well of being.

ə.

Spiritual experiences and phenomena are a very important stage in the process. Important because unless one has them it is very difficult to go beyond them, to pierce the illusoriness of all experience or retire the desire to have them. These experiences should be embraced but constantly resubmitted to the Essential, which will eventually lead the practitioner to the clear understanding that spiritual experiences have no more to do directly with spirituality than hair color or the particular weather patterns on any given day.

Spiritual phenomena are a part of existence, but no more nor less than that. All phenomena are no more nor less than that.

There is only one transcendent Reality, and on its heels come the consequences. Reality is simply and utterly absent of features; devoid of quality, form, and substance. Everything that can be experienced or identified with is a consequence of this Reality. To confuse the consequences with the Truth is the essence of all illusion.

૨ૐ

There is a great deal of intellectually-based dharma floating around which requires a particular kind of discrimination to detect. Just reworked, rechewed, refried dharma beans which some-one said once who had an actual view, but then others take what they think that meant and use the words to play dharma scrabble and make up and rearrange words in a way that makes an interesting and time-consuming game of the whole thing and is pleasing to the intellect. But in terms of actual experience . . . there is no longer any thread to the living force of radical realization. It takes a refined sense to be able to tell the difference. The language used can be almost exactly the same. One has to become like a master jeweler with a developed eye and the instinct for telling a highly polished stone from an actual gem. There is a lot of costume jewelry out there —empty rhetoric that looks and sounds good and is great for sport-ing at a party or in print but wouldn't get you more than a couple of minutes of interest at the pawn shop. Only the real can tell the fake, not the fake the real.

Time will tell or, more accurately, actions will tell how much of what is being spouted out here is just intellectual extrapolation on a little bit of experience as opposed to the real thing. It's something to watch for. It's hard to imagine that all of this could just be intellectual when words like "shattered," "destroyed," "annihilated" just keep coming up as the only words that are even close to expressing the inner feelings and experiences that are occurring. But then again, of all the features most supremely developed in the human race, the capacity to fool oneself ranks chief among them. So the whole consideration is worth keeping in one's sights.

&

When we observe the collection of things that we attribute to part of the package of self long enough and intimately enough, at some point we realize, that's all there is! There is no more than that. There is only "just this." At that point, any idea of being someone, anyone, having any identity, having a self, becomes laughable, and obviously crazy. We live asleep. The nature of this sleep is that we don't see all that we are in the moment, and in that unconsciousness live with this conditioned sense of being someone who is something beyond all the manifestations we think we are associated with. But to become present and pass out of denial requires a passionate and intimate investigation of the psychological self, the body/mind, an investigation which takes one right to the limits of it, so all of it is seen and known. The revelation that ensues once all one's manifestations are seen and known is simply the revelation of the absence of the self. The acknowledged absence of self is the womb in which the true Self is conceived and born. The Self is the presence of absence.

&

Consciousness gives us a view of Reality much the way an x-ray works. The energy of the x-ray passes through what is just on the surface and reveals the essential structure, the bones, on which the fleshy details of the organism are hung. Consciousness is exactly like this. When we use a highly refined awareness to see through what is on the surface, however, its power penetrates Everything, revealing Nothing; going and going, moving on and on without ever reflecting or revealing a single thing to our standard vision or senses. To use pure consciousness as a means of perception is to risk penetrating Reality beyond everything that the mind presently stands on and depends on for its "sanity." But only this perfectly surrendered form of seeing through, seeing past, and seeing beyond is worthy and reliable if we want to know, love, or serve God.

❧

There is only all these collected manifestations and phenomena that make up this particular body/mind—but there is no self associated with them. How could there be? Where is it? What is it? These questions are unanswerable not because they are particularly profound or because we haven't perfected our understanding enough to pluck the answer from the tree of Truth. These questions are unanswerable because the self does not exist! Simply that. There is only "what is." All the phenomena—all the things one can point at, can "prove" the existence of in form—come and go, change and are impermanent. That is obvious. What the mind refuses to do is to actually look for this thing called "self." If it did—truly look, that is —it would eventually find nothing and have a good belly laugh about the craziness of belief in and obedience to this imaginary self.

The mind is certainly a petty tyrant. It knows that if it gives us any room at all its whole authority will be undermined. That's why it hangs on so tightly, with such an iron grip. No dissent from its rule is tolerated. Once we see what it is doing, what it is buffering us from, then it's only a matter of time before we abandon it completely. The mind is completely useless for most aspects of living, yet it is running everything. It is like a power saw out of control. Running rampant and cutting the world up into little unconnected jagged pieces. The mind is useless for knowing Reality.

❧

The EEC (enlightened ego complex) is a condition in which, having had experiences and references for the awareness that only God is and that God is Everywhere and that one is just present in His field of Reality, the "I" then takes the symptoms or effects or phenomena that accompany those experiences and makes up a story about them that stations the ego at the center and as the cause of God's doing. When not referenced to a state of God being Everywhere, bigger than one and containing one, we take the memory of the state and ego uses it to pretend that *it* is God, it is enlightened, it is Everything. This gets a 5 star (*****) rating on the HAH! scale and needs to be fully exposed, understood, seen for what it is. The EEC is, in fact, just another manifestation of God. It's what ego does, it's what ego is for—and it is just ego—a facet of God—who is infinitely greater, all consuming, beyond, and prior to the EEC.

❧

Consciousness must expand to infinity. It lawfully seeks to do this. But mind contracts and attempts to limit consciousness, and internally we are at the effect of this war. We have captured an eagle, confined it to a fish bowl, and wonder at its foul mood.

Consciousness can only expand into God. God is the only substance in the universe which acts as a conductor for consciousness. Therefore, in order for consciousness to expand, that which we would like consciousness to expand toward must become recognized as God for us. When absolutely everything is seen as God, then consciousness moves there—takes up residence there—happily, easily, and lawfully.

We, however, would like our consciousness to expand without giving up our dualistic ideas of right and wrong, good and bad, left and right; and this is impossible. When the perception of "not God" invades our heart, there our consciousness is truncated, walled off, penned in to suffer the smallness of a personal and private life, a compartmentalized world of separateness, disconnection, and fragmentation.

૨૦

Regardless of the experience that Being may have, even the direct knowledge of God, mind just keeps doing what it has always done, and in the same way. You can't teach an old dog new tricks; you can just give him audiences to perform for where he can do no harm. You've got to retire him without letting him know you've retired him, give him something to do. The persistence and consistency of the mind is amazing. It just keeps coming back over and over again. We may believe that each time we manage to touch an expanded awareness and consciousness it will be easier to sustain such an awareness, or that mind will be a little less strong and all-identifying. This is true on one level, but on another level, it's either mind or God. And when it's mind, it makes no difference what kind of great experiences and references one has under one's belt, it's separation and the same old game. So the test is supreme. In order to finish this job, one's intention appears to have to be unfathomably unwavering and resolute; undistractible. How much does it really mean to us? is the question we will always be asked, and we have to answer by putting our blood, body, and bone into *action.*

ॐ

The whole path is the perfection of nothing. How to rest in surrender to any and every manifestation of the Divine which exists in the universe, including all of those manifestations which stream through the body/mind, and simultaneously stay rooted in the reality of our nothingness?

By being with "what is."

To completely be with "what is" is to simultaneously be undistractibly aware of what is *not.* Ego is that which is not. Ego, "me" and "I" are all exactly the same. We must give up the idea that ego is a healthy or unhealthy structure. Either consideration is just one side of the same illusion. Ego is neither good nor bad, right nor wrong, healthy nor unhealthy. It is simply not. Ignorance exists, which creates the impression that there is a separate ego, but behind that ignorance, ego is just a phantom. Exclusive identification with all the illusions which make up ego is exactly what gives the appearance that ego actually exists. If we begin to see what does actually exist, then we will begin to have a reference point from which to observe this un-reality.

Some "I" somewhere that exists separate from all else "is not." To see that, we have to see "what is" uninterruptedly with no tension. Then what "is not" becomes absolutely obvious.

ॐ

Pure consciousness is completely undefended. It is so open, so inclusive, so vulnerable that there is literally nothing to which it would, or could, guard itself against being in relationship. As a result, one who immerses himself or herself in the realm of pure consciousness also becomes completely undefended and vulnerable to the full breadth of the Reality of existence; to the Truth of All that is.

The common fear or misconception is that such vulnerability is dangerous, unwise, and contrary to physical survival. It is entirely necessary that the one who establishes himself in the Vision of All does so in the Heart, but in everyday life he remains armed with a tremendous range of refined distinctions and worldly wisdom. This is no paradox, but a marriage of extraordinary measure that leaves the one who is the seat of this marriage in the position we could call "enlightened duality."

ཨ

There he is again this morning in meditation, the man who is trying to surrender in just the right way so that he can disappear. An entire hour dedicated to this effort and the mirage is just as solid as ever. This is God's greatest mischief: that the effort to transcend oneself is, in the end, the exact and very effort that perpetuates the illusion that one is at all. When there is nothing to transcend, only "what is," and there never was anyone to begin with at all—never anyone separate, never any one there—what will the effort (to remove what is not) create? Madness. The kind of madness one can see any day of the week on the street, on a television, in a newspaper, at the mall. "I" am the effort to handle the problem of me. Everything "I" have been and am about as a separate individual, personality, and ego is exactly a product of all the efforts to improve the condition of that "I", or in this case to progress "spiritually."

If we think we can do this by ourselves, we're not trying hard enough. If we haven't surrendered to Help, it's because we think we can do it on our own. We must get on with doing it on our own so that we can find out once and for all if that is true. Any version of "I could do it if I wanted to," or "As soon as I get around to making the effort things are going to change," never got anybody anything, anywhere, anytime, ever.

There is only realization. No progress. No possibility of becoming anything different. No change. Nothing, nothing, nothing that one can do. Surrender cannot be "done" either. One day, suddenly, it just is. Surrender is nothing more than effort having finally outgrown itself.

৵

The self is an impossibility. As a limited, separate, not-part-of-everything-else self, we can forget about it. That we think there is such a self is only a lazy, unexamined habit. The Reality is very obvious, but we have been conditioned completely out of, beyond, and past the obvious to the imagined self in which we parade around in despair and confusion. There is just "what is." How could there ever be any unhappiness in that? In fact, there cannot be. This is the gift of God, just this fact. This Truth, this imperishable Reality, is our innocence. Without just "what is" being rediscovered, we spend the rest of our lives in the habit of pasting a "self" on top of the obvious. Radical reliance on God is the only way to re-encounter the Truth. It would simply never occur to us because it is too close, too near to us already. We are rooted in seeking, and all seeking is to look far away. Even looking a millionth of an inch away is seeking, and that is far enough away to miss exactly where we are, which is the only place God can take us. Right here. Right now. Just this.

৵

"Just this" refers very specifically and blatantly to the type of perception that is required to live the Truth. Normally we graft this thing called "ego" onto "just this," interpreting it in a way which further defines and solidifies our sense of self, reinforcing it through the process of referencing "just this" to the illusion we nurture. We pretend there is someone there who exists apart from what "just is," and then assess what impact our interpretation will have upon this illusory creature that we call ourselves, that exists somewhere (we don't really know where), at some time (we don't really know when). We then either find "happiness" or misery in our perception of what this means to the illusory one we have made up.

It is simply evident and obvious that "just this" is all there is. There is no more, anywhere, at any time. There is only "just this." If there is "just this," there is nothing else, no other, no one to reference "just this" against, toward, or about.

So, yes, there is a movie playing, and we are disturbed by it, put off balance, lost to our true Self in it. But we keep trying to break into the projection room to sabotage the machine, or we obsessively plot ways we could assassinate the projectionist, or we file a lawsuit against the theater, entering into endless debate over whose fault it is that we are so miserable, when in actuality all we have to do is withdraw the screen so that no matter what gets projected, there is nothing for the drama to reflect off of. This is the one and only thing we have control over. It is actually quite simple to do but, in our misunderstanding, it's the last option that occurs to us.

⁊⦿

In our "normal" waking state there is an interpretation of all experience going on that is virtually impossible to catch. This interpretation pastes over pure consciousness and attaches all sorts of conditioning to it that leads us to draw conclusions about "reality." These conclusions are what comprise our beliefs about life and self. The reason these conditionings seem to be proven by our experience is that we miss the point at which we jump from the actuality of the experience to the adding in of the conditioned attachments. They get thrown into the soup while our back is turned, and then we mistake this spoiled recipe for life as it really is. Meditation is the practice of not turning one's back on this dynamic, but observing it instead, until one day our awareness is sharp enough to keep the soup from being contaminated by the mind's sloppy habits.

&

Consciousness is pure energy which has no boundary and is related to Everything. Everything that appears to us in matter only seems to exist in relationship to the tool with which we are perceiving it: mind. The mind experiences only one very finite and limited layer of reality, the layer called "matter" and "the world." Other forms of perception, awareness, and consciousness do not "see" this layer of reality. From the vantage point of these other forms of perception, this layer does not, in fact, exist. It is only the limitation of an individual's consciousness which creates the illusion that something exists. The only way to experience this truth directly is to surrender the dictatorship of the mind to faith in God and Truth. If one allows grace to do its work, it will undermine and deliver one from the illusion that one is bound to through dedication to the mind and its limited form of perception.

The consistent practice of meditation is absolutely key and crucial to letting this process mature into something more solid and reliable than a flash of insight or chance upper-world experience. Meditation can be used as a bridge to introduce this level of consciousness into one's daily life and to empower practices which can anchor a fully awakened, fully integrated awareness that lives, breathes, and acts in the world.

# THE WAY OF THE BODY

When the whole body is experienced all at once, not just by the mind, which can only experience one part at a time, all the feelings and sensations that are present in the body balance each other out. An appropriate feeling relationship to the full body delivers our attention to a natural harmony that allows consciousness to penetrate into a much subtler level of awareness.

Mind, however, by definition, can only experience or observe that which is separate. Mind is only a processor, a device through which that which is separate can be registered, tallied, compared, and compartmentalized. Mind is not good for anything else. Because mind does not want to be extinguished, does not want to be useless and without a function, it thrives on separation, and perpetuates separation in order to ensure its own legitimacy.

To experience the whole body all at once sets the entire body vibrating at the same rate, the same frequency, moving to and fro in the same wave. This we call integrity. When integrity is achieved in the body—that is, when the whole body is experienced all at once—there is no longer any war going on between parts of that body: no parts are moving against each other or existing at odds with each other. At this point, the "parts" literally cease to exist, since the only thing that creates separation or a sense of distinct parts in the first place is when their timing is discontinuous, some parts moving left while others go right, some rising up while others pull down. When there is integrity between the parts, what we commonly experience as feeling and sensation within the body becomes impossible. All gross feeling and sensation, and therefore all experience, is the result of parts moving contrary to each other—nothing more. When the parts move contrary to each other, they pull on our attention and demand our awareness. We become aware of the friction that exists at the boundary between the out-of-sync elements. This is the exact basis of self-referencing. Attention called away from Context, away from the unbounded awareness that results from complete continuity between parts, is what self-referencing is.

Spiritual practices are for the purpose of harmonizing the human machine in such a way that there is no tension. When there is a-tension, or attention, and only unity of the psychophysical apparatus, then consciousness is utterly free to rest in God, in the context of Divine nothingness, of no perception, no idea, no experience. If we observe clearly, we can see the inner war, the battle and the division, that results internally in our psyche and physiology when we fail to practice the basics of kindness, generosity, and compassion. The practice of kindness, generosity, and compassion is the foundational practice for creating the inner bodily harmony which is the basis of liberation itself, the cornerstone of the way to discover who we really are: no one and nothing.

The human body, experienced all at once as it is, *is* the entire universe. Containing everything, nothing is foreign or set apart from it at that point. Conscious perception of the human body all at once brings about a particular kind of miracle in which the body then exists as a microcosm of the entire universe and everything can be known within it.

~

After dinner tonight, triggered by a single small incident, the giant force of "NO" came to visit. It started with an insignificant event and quickly gathered steam and momentum; rolling into a "NO" to everything and everyone; severe, violent, final. It just took over the mind, and it was everything that the body could do to prevent this "NO" from expressing itself outwardly as everyone else's problem. It was burning inside, cooking from the inside out.

Extremely wild and reactive thoughts were marching through the mind, creating problems, seeing difficulties, injustices, wrongs that must be righted, and on and on and on. All this while the body attempted to direct all of this energy into the simple task of doing the dishes.

It wasn't until showering at bedtime that the mind let itself be beaten, taken apart by its own misery, and admitted its own helplessness in the face of the force of "no." Then, out of the dirt of this helplessness, came the flower of faith. How far the mind has to get pushed before it will take refuge in the Absolute, in God. Suffering is vital to this whole process! Without it we simply will never resort to taking refuge in faith, and without faith we're simply going to rely on what has always worked before; namely, our strategies and habits that bring us some comfort or pleasure. When no distraction is an option for us anymore in the face of the pain of being human, we have the possibility of taking refuge in faith. Faith allows us to enter the pain that can transform our entire work. There is so much energy in our pain. But it is so hard to embrace. We so mechanically and habitually run from pain, avoid feeling it.

What came out of opening up to so much pain was the direct understanding that everything done and tied up until now in this life has been a strategy to get love. All the skills, talents, abilities, and successes have been developed because the mind thinks it will capture love through them. But these strategies have all failed, many times over. According to the conditioning and belief system of this culture, they should have worked, they should have brought love by now, but they haven't and they don't. The only thing that has been untried is actually loving others, one to one, in consistent, ordinary, and concrete ways. Serving people directly is the only thing left untried in the quest for love. There is the risk of loving, or nothing at all.

ès

We must be willing to let this body/mind go, freely represent its destiny as an animal/human on the face of the planet, discharge the overriding editor who is continually derailing our natural participation as a human being in this life, and at that point make the crucial distinction about who we really are and leave the rest of it alone. We must let what is personal and psychological find its own natural integrity by totally accepting it—no denial, just responsiveness and aliveness in the present moment—and stop giving it (the body/mind) a hard time, stop second-guessing it, stop interrupting its ups and downs, its natural tendencies, its ability to be ordinary, and from that place look at the Reality of things. This is what is needed, instead of trying to impose some extraordinary imagined reality of a "conscious person" onto the subjectively immersed, already conditioned human one, who has a very specific life to live, full of trials, tribulations, and imperfections.

ès

Strictly speaking, obedience on the spiritual path is obedience to one's elder, the spiritual Teacher. Eventually, however, once the practitioner's body itself has been trained in the discipline of spiritual practice into which the Teacher has initiated the student, obedience begins to take the form of following what the body knows, its intuition and instinct in the course of everyday life. It is only the radical willingness with which the student practices obedience to these bodily instructions that can allow God's will to consume and deconstruct ego's cohesiveness. When obedient, one cannot rest in any type of thought or strategy about who or how one should be. It is left up to God, and whatever He prompts must be embraced. This can show up as a need for warriorship when it does not behoove or gratify ego to act with ferocity and vigilance. It can also look like kindness and compassion toward someone when the rest of the world is forming a lynch mob for the very same fellow.

If we are obedient, with the grace of God as our only faith and guide, we may let our life march on without us; we may surrender into the perfect flow of "what is" without any desire to control, predict, manage, maintain, arrange, secure, or manipulate circumstances and others to any end beyond what the Divine would have occur, be it nothing or everything, be it criminal or holy, be it exciting or boring, risky or safe, understandable or cryptic. To let go into the stream of this very life is the greatest ecstasy possible. It is the only liberation. To participate the way God would have us participate, on His terms, according to His wishes and dictates, with no life of our own, is the highest possibility for human life.

2&

If you say to the average person that they need to trust everything, totally, one hundred percent, they immediately go into a panic just thinking about all the situations and people they do not, or would not, feel safe with, rather than expanding trust to include their own sense of what and who to avoid, what is harmful, toxic, or dangerous. Trust is the willingness to act on what one feels to be true, that's all. It doesn't mean setting oneself up to be taken advantage of, mugged in a dark alley, or emotionally hung out to dry. The word "trust" is so polluted in our culture that it would benefit us to coin a new word that has fresh meaning and start again.

To trust is to act from one's own understanding with confidence. The form of the action may not look at all like the standard connotations of what is "trusting," or it may go way beyond the standard. The point is to develop faith in the feeling sense that accompanies one's relationship to God and evolution itself. Such faith is demonstrated by a willingness to act based on that sense and then to gradually accept whatever consequences arise as a result of that action.

રકુ

It seems that for God to know Himself through the vehicle of human form (which is exactly and precisely what human beings have been made for) takes no time at all, is outside of time, and does not depend upon or consider time. For the same human form to mature into a *manifest* reflection of God's grace seems to take a lot of time, requires time, occurs in time. Why shouldn't it? The body/mind itself only occurs and exists in time; therefore, it must play the game by and through time. But grace and God do not heed or play in time. Consciousness can participate instantly. The body is slow to follow. This is where the Work lies.

A human being is the tangent point where time and no-time cross paths. A human being lives with the necessity of becoming skilled at forever balancing on the tightrope of this paradox.

રકુ

Let's talk about habits. Now there are habits and there are habits. Good habits, bad habits, even harmless habits, perhaps. But the habit of ego is the big habit. Bigger than big. Bigger than the biggest ever. Ego is an extremely huge, persistent habit. Even the clear and direct experience that ego is only an idea, a practiced position, a

94

laziness of the mind, is not enough to clear the habit, because the habit is in the body, not in the mind. We have to get our body's full cooperation and attention, not just be able to control the mind long enough to have a burst of right thinking.

Disintegration is what would occur without this habit. Ego is what is holding everything together. Ego is the implosion, the contraction that holds attention captive and mean in a tiny location, imprisoning us. No wonder we're all in a bad mood. This disintegration of the self and integration into the Self is the natural tendency and desire of God—and would occur if we surrendered the cramp of ego, which is all ego is: the attempt to hold together and limit what is essentially expansive and limitless in nature.

❧

When consciousness first awakens to Reality, to the actual nonexistence of self, the nervous system of the body may "crash." Since its orientation toward reality is suddenly removed, no longer has any foundation, it must rewire itself in a completely new way, to a whole new structure and dynamic. Such a crash can even be felt as horrifying, but not the traditional form of horror, not the horror that comes from being repulsed by something; rather the horror one would experience if something the size of the Empire State Building were to suddenly disappear before one's very eyes; the horror of the unreliability of mind and its perceptions.

❧

Anger comes like a storm, unannounced: as an unexpected embrace of passion that steals the full attention away in an instant; as when one's lover suddenly arrives and one finds oneself unexpectedly giddy, all awash in joy. We must take care not to involve other humans in the aftermath of anger's effect on us, people who are not only undeserving but who are also unable to ground this lightning back to earth without getting singed and burned by our misdirected loosings of a force which is clearly only provided as a magic carpet that we might ride right up to God, into relationship with God, if we weren't so habitually and ignorantly misusing it: stealing it from the temple and spending it in the marketplace.

Needing to act out these emotions and feelings is just the inability to hold what can be called "creative tension," God's very gift. It's exactly the same as thinking that one is obligated to orgasm because there is a loud buzz happening in the genitals.

&

Relationship calls forth every area of one's failure to practice. All the failures that we can easily keep hidden from ourselves in isolation, all the ideas about how and who we are that we cherish between our own two ears, all these must be subjected to the army of Reality which marches in perfect time with human relationship. It is invaluable to be in a relationship and get direct and immediate feedback on where we really are able to walk our talk and where we are not—on where we really stand with respect to the practice of kindness, generosity, compassion, surrender, and all other spiritual ideas, concepts, and teachings.

&

My friend is a good example of someone who is willing to do what is wanted and needed without thinking about what is in it for her—what she will get out of it. My personality, on the other hand, in most moments and circumstances calculates what it is that it can gain for itself, and this often takes the form of looking for a payoff in terms of the "spiritual" work it is doing. How twistedly self-centered can you get? What would it be like to take exactly what was wanted and needed for and by others as the only thing that mattered with regard to one's spiritual life?

In the fireplace today there was a red hot fire that had reduced a cedar log to ashes. What would produce a hot enough fire in life to reduce all of what is in between one and God to the same kind of ash? Service perhaps. Relentless service with no thought of self, no self-reference, no idea of need for self; just service. Now there's a Reality check. It certainly puts the need or value of having "wonderful experiences" in an interesting perspective.

&

The opportunity to be in clear, simple, wholesome, loving, playful relationship with another human being; this is the reward of being with children. What a welcome and extreme demand and gift! There is nothing like being with the kids. Our only job is to make sure they win in the relationship, to make sure that it is they who draw us into their world and not the other way around. But that is seldom the case. Usually (only because we're bigger and more sophisticated in our manipulative capabilities), we win, dragging them kicking and screaming, literally or at least psychically, into our world—into the insanity of our own 21st-century-virtual-reality-get-it-quick-and-easy-and-just-the-way-we-want-it world.

Go out in public, look around, and you will see a world full of people who have completely lost their curiosity, their desire to explore, to know, to experiment, to ask questions, to innovate. They do things the way the person in front of them in line is doing things without a question. They have been thoroughly broken and "tamed" into doing things the way someone else (their parents) wanted them done, and their ability to think and invent for themselves has completely atrophied. And of course all marketing executives are thrilled by this. What an easy job all the big corporations have after this early training. All they have to do is put out enough advertising, telling all the sheep, "This is the way you do things around here, what you buy, what you wear, what you need to be," and presto, the sheep go right into the queue for their Guess jeans or whatever.

If we practice self-observation when we are with our children we may be surprised by the amount of time we spend "leading the witness." What kind of insanity are we perpetuating when we always try to get our children to do things our way? Children are just naturally brilliant, there's no getting around it. They see. To destroy that seeing, and subsequently their ability to respond to their world, in favor of our own conditioning and reactions, is much, much worse than what is going on in the rainforest. The kind of diversity we are annihilating when we do this is at least as detrimental to the evolutionary potential and survival of the planet as destruction of the rainforest is.

It is not being suggested here that one should not create boundaries and introduce discipline into the lives of the children for whom they care. The suggestion is that the boundaries we are currently enforcing are to some degree, or a great degree, arbitrary and based on our own need to prop up the neurosis that manifests as our own habitual control of our environment and those around us; a control which makes that environment less threatening and easier to deal with because it remains familiar and limited to a range of forms we are accustomed to handling.

An example is the underlying charge with which we discipline our children for inappropriate behavior in public because we feel embarrassed and ashamed as a result of the looks that get shoveled our way by other members of the child-intolerant public—looks which transport us instantly back to the time when we were little kids and were shamed ourselves for innocent and naturally childish behavior. The essential motivation behind our discipline is actually, "Look, Johnny. I'm a thirty-eight-year-old man with twelve employees, a successful business, and money in the bank. I've worked long and hard at creating the illusion of being an adult for myself and I will not be reduced to experiencing feelings that make me feel all of three years old again in the company of other strangers by your behavior." And then we proceed to shut our kids down and shame them in precisely the same way we were shamed, and if we squint just right and use only a tiny bit of imagination we can already see their future grown-up bodies steamrolling the innate capacities of their own children in another twenty years, and on it will go. Perhaps we are always "nice" and "sweet" with our children and therefore do not even consider that we may be "steamrolling," but to give children the idea, through one's modeling of it, that they should be "nice" all the time is just as much steamrolling them as yelling at them to do it our way would be.

Steamrolling includes all the layers upon layers of mechanically delivered instructions that we pass off as boundary making—instructions that are no more than the way we do it and the way our parents did it, which we translate into "the way it is done!" And in this mechanical, invisible to ourselves, download of advising, moralizing, distribution of artificial ethics, and unexamined opinions it never dawns on us that the radiant and unfettered intelligence of the child, when given the freedom and space to do so, will experiment with his or her world in such a way that they will arrive at the most intelligent method of interacting with the world in its current condition, given the impossibility of that child's acting outside of the bounds of his or her own authentic astuteness, joy, spontaneity, and inherently social nature. That is unless we treat them like one of Pavlov's dogs and ring the little "I love you" bell every time they do it our way, or slide them a little—even subtle—dirty look every time they do something differently, even if brilliantly. If we do this, over time they will cease to be responsive to their environment because they will be too busy trying to be responsive to us: our preferences, likes, dislikes, and neurotic habits, having been trained into focusing on us because if they don't do it right they'll be denied their number one priority in life, the security in love they need to survive.

If they are secure in our love—the unconditionalness of it—they will be radically free to respond to life with the innate intelligence and suppleness of mind with which they were born. If they are scared of losing this first foundation in life, our love, then that intelligence and suppleness will dedicate itself to, and rigidify around, the necessity of securing that love. This is the fundamental dynamic which produces all forms of human neurosis, psychosis, and psychological imbalance. To some extent, and it is true of all of us to a greater or lesser degree, a portion of our faculties which are designed to interface with Reality in a free and evolutionary way are instead retarded into the service of ensuring a base level of support which our parents should have provided for us naturally and abundantly in the very early stages of our lives. We all know how much time we spend projecting our mothers and fathers onto all the other "adults" in our environment and then trying to manipulate the circumstances in such a way that we get the acknowledgment, approval, recognition, and praise that we still feel we are missing deep down.

So the next time we catch ourselves telling our children what to think, feel, do, say, or be, we might just have a little look inside and see if we can catch the mood in there. Are our promptings and directives coming from a mood of fear? Are they coming from some version of the thought, "My god, if I don't socialize this animal right now it's going to grow up shunned by society, a lost and lonely soul (just like me)"? We might ask if we are willing to be a demonstration of what we consider to be a functional, happy human being and trust that the children in our care will absorb into their very cells exactly what we really are, piece by piece, step by step, and naturally and effortlessly grow into mature, socially capable adults in their own time and way. Or we might ask if we would rather demonstrate the behavior of a frightened individual who, because he or she was never given the freedom to mature naturally in the presence of other mature adults themselves, must in turn force a barrage of rote behaviors and reactions upon his or her own children. If these conditionings are forced early enough in the process, they undermine the complex and ultimately profound process of experimentation and trial and error which produces truly wise, elegant, and bright human beings.

The more injunctions we pile on a child, the more conditioning, the more conditional hoops we demand they jump through on their way to hearty participation in life, the more neurotically the natural urge for gathering a complex array of impressions will manifest. Gathering these impressions must occur, and the easier we make the child's job of doing that the more his or her energy will go into the process of evolving as a human being. If children have all kinds of injunctions to hurdle and deal with, all their energy will be tied up in just getting past those obstacles, and they will grow up very cunning, clever, street smart, and manipulative, but very underdeveloped in the aspects for which God had planned a spectacular maturity for them; i.e., profound and satisfying relationships, passionate avenues to creativity, a capacity for wonder and worship, vulnerability and receptivity to the revelatory outpourings of the Divine itself.

ॐ

Grace is already flowing, has always been flowing, always will be flowing. There is a special kind of energy that is constantly on tap, available for free, just for the asking, but we have to have a machine that can use that kind of fuel. If the world suddenly, by international law, provided rocket fuel for free at every gas station on the planet, a lot of people who haven't thought it through would be running around saying, "Free rocket fuel! Great, now I can go to the moon!" But of course without the rocket, without building and owning a proper vehicle that can make use of that kind of fuel, nobody's going anywhere. So we just keep polishing our Camaro, Toyota, or Volvo and talking about the magnificence of rocket fuel without ever bothering to do the work it would require to build the vehicle that could make use of that fuel. That is personal work. God cannot do that for us. God is not a mechanic. He is the Chairman of the Board at the power company. Pure, raw, highest voltage energy. Plug into that all naive and starry-eyed and it's game over. Anybody with any sense, once they understand who God really is, will start scrambling for the parts they need to build a transformer. A machine that can take that energy, eat it, and be explosively moved without being destroyed. Now that would be the true and appropriate expression of gratitude. This is the problem with most self-service, do-it-yourself spiritual paths, books, and teachings. They keep talking about the rocket fuel, but very few recognize or provide appropriate guidelines for how to make use of the raw energy that God provides.

&

There are two ways to pay for this Work. The first way is all at once, in big gut-wrenching chunks. The other way to pay is in every moment possible, at every opportunity, choosing conscious sacrifice, delaying gratification whenever possible, in a million small ways, without fanfare, without looking like a hero, doing what's wanted and needed. Simple service.

❧

The question is: Are we willing to pass through this life in complete obscurity, unacknowledged and unrewarded for simply being who we are? People are only acknowledged for *what* they are, not *who* they are. To be acknowledged for what we are can never produce the deep satisfaction and the casefulness we seek and can find only after discovering who we are. What we are is just what we are. It is not great or wonderful or bad or twisted or perfect or exemplary or anything. It is just what we are. Once we know *who* we are, then we can let what we are be. That is the only Work worth doing, the only offering worth giving to the world. Yet we strut around trying to manipulate what we are to gain recognition for who we are, when who we are can never, and will never, be recognized except by those who know who they are and who certainly will not give our ego the attention it is trying to generate for itself based on what it is. Oh, the peace, the joy, the liberation of letting what we are be.

❧

All art is about individuation through surrender to Real expression. It takes ultimate courage to express ourselves in any form—through writing, art, music, relationship, parenting, or any other vocation—because at first we must be completely self-centered, uncaring of what anyone else thinks, expressing our own personal truth. This begins as pure indulgence in the first stage, full of ego and self, but if attention is paid, the same unwavering commitment to expression will reveal what the chosen form of communication itself wants to express. Over time, this can lead the artist toward the Absolute, and the self starts to get crowded out, pushed aside, overpowered, overshadowed by just expression, with no one doing the expressing. What starts out as the most selfish activity can become the most selfless if pursued with the right aim, intention, and Context.

೪

In the night my son wakes up yelling next to his sister. Not wanting her to be awakened as well, I angrily grab him and hold him close to quiet him. There, in the middle of the night, my son asks sadly, "Why did you do that, Daddy?" How can it be? Such professed devotion and surrender to You, and then, in the dead of night, the enactment of such reactive force on the body of my child? May the pain of action such as this become a permanent necessity to Remember You always. A single moment of forgetfulness is enough to commit grievous error.

೪

Pain is the inconsistency between action in life and what is known to be True. In the action of being rough with my son comes the proof that "I" is not One, but many. In one moment feeling the magnificence of God, in the next, stunned, shocked, and mortified by the ignorance and violence of these actions. How is this possible? To still be so unconscious that anger and irritation win over the needs of the children. The unitive is not yet running the show here, even though certain "profound" experiences are used by the mind to try and convince it otherwise. Something else is bigger than the commitment to act in alignment with what is known to be True. In

Reality, Truth is not "known" until it is represented consistently and reliably in action. There is ignorance not only of what is being acted out, but of what it is that is acting out. And without knowing what this is, the old protective devices still automatically interact with people in a way that empowers separation, not the love and service of Unity.

૪.

Practice only allows us to become an expression of the Divine in this world. It is not necessary. But it is necessary if we want to serve others. The work of having the experience of our Divinity is nothing compared to the work of being a worthy, reliable vehicle for the continuous expression of the Divine.

૪.

The interesting thing about experiences which have a lot of energy in them, like intense states of bliss or ecstasy, is that after the arising of such energy the unpurified aspects of other centers in the body often steal it to feed themselves. If we are not paying attention, or are not prepared to consciously interrupt this theft, we wind up suddenly extremely angry or irritated or enraged over something inconsequential. Refined energies can have a real destabilizing effect if one isn't vigilant and responsible for the habits and tendencies of one's entire mechanism. We must practice as hard as we can before a radical level of energy becomes available. Our current level of practice may not seem like a problem, and we may feel no greater urgency to practice than we currently have, but that is only because there is a limited amount of energy flowing through the system, compared to what it's like when states of union or rapture arise, for instance. The time to prepare for battle is now, not once the battle is at hand. That will be far too late. A prudent practitioner of this way should realize this.

‽

The process of breathing is a natural activity with a natural cycle. Most people "grab" air, inhaling breaths as though oxygen was on special, available for a limited time only. This overbreathing is stressful to the body and mind. "Inhale" should not even be a verb because it is not an activity that is to be done; it is the natural response to a diminished level of oxygen in the body. We don't have to push air out, it falls out—is relaxed out by the very design with which the body is born.

In a similar fashion, we do not "raise" the energy of kundalini.* It naturally springs heavenward when the mind "exhales,"—vacates the location at the top of the spine—and with that pressure released, kundalini ascends, like water gushing upward and out of an opened fire hydrant. But our relationship to thinking mirrors our relationship to our breath. We believe we can't get enough, and so we hold the breath of mentation and wonder why we feel so thrown out of whack, agitated, and uneasy.

In many ways we have the workings of the universe backwards. We are trained to believe that we have to be good, perfect, holy, balanced in order to get the grace of God. So we work hard to change ourselves to be good so we can gain the benediction of the Divine. In this scenario we are struggling to gain what it is that we were never able to wrangle from our parents. Our "being good" is

---

\* Kundalini - A powerful energy that resides at the base of the spine and can move up the spine spontaneously, especially when specific practices are engaged.

106

motivated by what we hope to receive; therefore, all our changes, actions, efforts, and even gestures of kindness are contaminated because they are full of self. We perform them to get something for ourselves. The truth is that God grants His or Her love to anyone who is willing to receive it, no matter what their condition, level of attainment, or willingness to abide by the moral, ethical, cultural, or so-called spiritual laws of the world. Once this love is received, nothing but goodness pours forth from such a person because they are without motivation for their action and interaction with the world. With God's love they are no longer bottomless, and become quickly filled. They are then freed into service, since they no longer need to serve themselves in any way. In fact, they no longer need anything.

"Freed into service" is different from "free to serve." Once the Divine has fully and irrevocably penetrated a person they are loosed, liberated into a realm in which there is no possibility other than service. Service is the lawful and unavoidable expression, destiny, and activity of such a person. There is no choice about it. They are freed into service but are not "free."

ॐ

In a vegetarian restaurant there were two women talking about some kind of workshop one of them had been doing. She was bragging glibly about leaving her body. To look at her face was to look at a scared, bitter, and lost person, grasping for something fulfilling.

There must be all sorts of people out there trying to leave their bodies, and succeeding, by stirring up their own psychosis and childhood trauma to the point of dissociation with human life, with a healthy and grounded ego. Because this is touted as something "spiritual," suddenly they have an identity which is grafted to the need to be psychotic so they can live out some insane notion of what transcendence is. "Leaving one's body" can happen in two ways: either through the denial of the body or through the full awareness of it. The first is dissociation. The second is super-association, where one becomes so associated with one's own body that one discovers the actual size, presence, and depth of that body to be infinitely more expansive than was ever imagined. Super-association makes us ecstatic in life, which is then our heaven. Dissociation only makes us crazy as hell.

か

How can one be responsive if one is not present with "what is"? When we are responsive—when we see things as they are and act in alignment with what we see—we can serve the evolutionary needs of Reality. We can impact the world. We can help others. But if we are not responding to "what is," our action is bound to be ineffective because the action will not be appropriate to or in sync with that which actually exists. "Well, of course," we may be thinking. But can we see the ways in which we act, not consistent to Reality but consistent to our *beliefs* about Reality and our beliefs about ourselves, and then pretend to be a victim and blame the rest of the world when things don't go smoothly or work out? Well, no matter what we think, the answer to that question is "no," we cannot see the veils we employ. Such is the proven reality of human psychology. Which is why we need help and support and feedback on the path. In some form, and the more traditional the better, we need the Buddha, the dharma, and the sangha. Otherwise, we shall bulldoze our way through life using a jackhammer when a feather duster would do, traveling by boat when we need a plane, whispering when we need to shout, trusting sharks when we need a Teacher, and defending ourselves against those who truly love us when we need to receive that very love.

ॐ

Participation in life is really the key. It's the only way we get to test and strengthen and build the kind of vehicle that is necessary to live a life that can embody, hold, or transmit Divine Influence. Without participation and the opportunity for a lot of trial and error with the use of one's own energy in all forms of relationship, everything is only conceptual guesswork. Got to get it out there, take the risks, take the falls, get up again, and hone the ability to interface with the world. Death will come soon enough; then we can relax and enjoy infinite free time, not having to do anything. Until then, better work our ass off so death isn't hell. Life is the place where we can learn to navigate skillfully in hell before we get there. Life is practice for hell. Knowing how to handle oneself perfectly in hell is the only heaven there is.

ॐ

There is the relaxation of body: the muscles, the tendons, the organs; then there is the relaxation of the psyche, in which one can actually feel the mind releasing its grip on molecules of thought and desire; and beyond that, there is the relaxation of spirit itself—expanding and dissolving into Infinity. The Work is about realizing a level of relaxation of spirit and, through practice, allowing that quality of relaxation to work its way back out, penetrating the outer layers of manifestation, back through the psyche and then to the physical body itself. This is the basis of enlightened duality. Where some traditions would end with the final full relaxation of spirit—with consciousness merging with Reality—other traditions only begin, and call for the penetration of this relaxation back to the grossest layers of manifestation. The body, mind, and spirit must be retrained, almost like a newborn, to become fully active while in this surrendered state. This is what Zen refers to as "effortless effort." To realize this and anchor it in the body is the Work.

ஃ

voidance with respect to human relationship is a-void-dance. A void dance is specifically appropriate to describe a relationship in which the feminine or the masculine attempts to live in isolation, separate from the influence of the other quality. It is one partner trying to dance alone, without the other. It is pure Context or Content refusing to allow the alchemical transformation to occur that would result from embracing, honoring, and revering the other pole of the existential dynamic. The masculine believes that Context is all that is important, all there is, and that saying "Yes" to Content would be a dangerous descent into loss of Context. The feminine, embodied in and completely identified with Content, fears the same. While establishing Context is crucial, it is absolutely, and literally, nothing on its own. And Content on its own is like a fine wine which must be held and contained in the empty glass before it can be shared or enjoyed. This is the entire basis of tantra. Heaven and earth in ecstatic play. Yin and yang. This is why relationship between a practicing man and woman is so crucial and core to the tantric path. It is exactly there that the man and woman learn the entire art of tantric life and are then able to apply this principle to their entire existence, whether alone or together. The masculine is under the illusion that Context can relate to the feminine through silence, long intense gazes, and the stark austerity of practice and discipline. But this is only how Context relates to *itself*. If we want the full manifestation of Reality, we must leave our game, our world, and enter the domain of the Other. But tender words, physical touch, and the demonstration through action of human love frightens the masculine, confuses it, undermines its grip on its idea about Truth. Men have to become that which is a living invitation for Content to enter into Context in order to free themselves from the limitations of un-embodied life.

≥

Feeling everything that a human body can feel is the bridge to feeling beyond the body. But the body must be embraced. Every nuance of its simple, ordinary, and subtle sensations and feelings must be reveled in, seen as holy, given full welcome, and dived into. Our path is one of radical embodiment—the courage to feel everything that is related to human life. This is our catapult to true spirituality. Then how can there be a fall? Then it will All be known. If no stone is left unturned along the way, what rock will the monster crawl out from beneath? Saying "Yes" to it all is the only way. Going beyond any idea of what we should be feeling, and instead experiencing and being with the actuality of what we are, is the Truth in the body and through the body. This is the Way.

≥

The feeling of being something or someone always comes from the past. Any "qualities" or "accomplishments" that one wants to take credit for and call "I" are only what has occurred as a result of keeping the "I" out of the way. To take credit for any good that sometimes prevails or creates itself through us is just ridiculous. When "I" is there, the space is vacant of possibility, love, magic. When "I" is nothing, miracles occur, and like wind chimes being blown in the wind, there can be sublime music, but there is no one doing it. What else could a human being want to live for than to be in the presence of the eternal creativity and play of God?

When we surrender to the needs of everyone and everything in the moment and hold possibility, our own creativity is supported by an unseen and dynamically reliable source which allows us to creatively accommodate far more variables than we ever imagined could be simultaneously entertained.

The "freedom" we habitually defend and claim for ourselves, whatever form that takes, pales in comparison to the liberation that results from surrendering to what is wanted and needed.

ﻋ

This spiritual Work is a reverse birth. In childbirth something big grows inside the body and then exits out near the base of the spine. In spiritual birth, something big also grows in the body, but then must transition upward through the top of the body. The heart may be equated with the cervix in this analogy, and there is a "crowning" stage in which, as this new being passes through it, the heart must stretch immeasurably beyond its previous capacity to accommodate the birth. As any mother will attest, this process is as excruciatingly painful as it can be Divine, blissful, and transcendent.

ﻋ

When we are writing out of our passion for God, we are being asked to write with His eyes, as He would see it if He had access to our vantage point. If we are successful in this pursuit, our vantage point becomes accessible to Him and feeds Him, feeds His Work. We must be willing to consider that being a devotee is nothing but actually being Him from a distinct vantage point that no one else has. This is the only truth of individuality. Mature individuality is not about being separate, it is about having a distinct vantage point within the Context of union. To be responsible for this vantage point is to declare the Truth from this vantage point without any degree of attachment to the vantage points we have clung to from our past and our previous conditionings. Part of being objective as a writer is that we create the event through our declaration of it. As a wise man once said, "If it's not written down, it never happened." This means that it's only when an occurrence is consciously digested by an individual as food for the Work—only when the event is interpreted or brought to the Context of the Work—that it exists as a moment of Truth. Until then it is nothing. It is only from the position of radical reliance on God that we can digest these impressions in a way that transforms them and makes them Real. Until then everything that happens is just a shadow. Nothing is real until the Lord witnesses it and calls it. We are being asked to be His eyes and call a world of Work impressions into existence through the practice of writing.

This occurs by making powerful or core distinctions. Powerful distinctions are those that pull an extremely specific and limited reality into the foreground while leaving everything else in the background. In relationship to writing, these distinctions become powerful through what we exclude from our writing more than through what we include. When we exclude everything extraneous to the core distinction, that distinction is made powerfully for others. If we attach other baggage to the distinction, it lacks power because it is clouded by sentimentality.

૨&

Our habits are not us. They need to be seen as they are without identification, and then we may decide to work with them, just as objectively and distantly as one may choose to weed a garden or care for a stray animal. We don't have to work with them at all. God doesn't love us any less due to the lack of training of our machine. We are perfect and whole and alive just as we are. The karma of our machine is distinct and fully at the effect of itself and its history. If we observe its reality objectively, there may be a spontaneous response to work with it in some way. Or there may not be. We must trust the Influence to determine that.

❧

The human body is the crucible in which a boggling array of experiments, transformations, reactions, and alchemy may take place. It is the most complicated, sophisticated, and delicate instrument God has ever created and has a very specific function and purpose: to transmute the substance of form back into formlessness, to reflect what it is that is God—that God has created—back to God; to give God a means to reabsorb the formed aspects of His creation so that He may create again, since this infinite play is His ultimate nature.

This is what a human being is evolved to do; has been made and designed for. The vast percentage of those who inhabit this vehicle (the human body) have absolutely no idea of this possibility and are being led through a life not only with a lack of cultural training but, even worse, with bad training which is completely contradictory to the ultimate functioning of this organism. The way in which we are taught to operate this machinery confounds it, ties it up in knots, throws its timing out of whack, and disharmonizes all of its systems.

❧

The primary hurdle or hindrance to conscious parenting is the trap of trying to parent differently from who we actually are. This seems contradictory to "conscious" parenting, but if we are not being with our children *as we are,* we will only create damage where we wanted to create happy whole humans. What kind of damage? The most fundamental damage that we ourselves suffer from: the belief that we are not okay.

Of course, parenting from who we actually are requires that we know who we actually are, and that is a big question. Maybe only a lifetime of investigation will yield up who we actually are, but this must be our approach, our aim. Parenting as we are does not mean that we don't honor the practices of not shaming, not making artificial boundaries, not abusing. It means that we rest in ourselves as the basic demonstration of conscious behavior and stop trying to parent perfectly as an extension of the neurotic and unconscious habit of trying to earn love by being something other than what we already are. If this basic cramp is released, our children will get us. Until then they only get a lie. No matter how appropriate or polished or knowledgeable that lie is, it is a shadow which will get passed on as shadow. Being outwardly as we are inwardly transmits the brightness of what it truly means to be human. If our expression of ourselves defies our beingness, the very basis of unconscious parenting will remain intact and hidden from view, the essential communication in this instance being, "I'm not okay as I am."

۞

As human beings, our daily life or practice in the body is the chamber where the soul is built. Eventually, once the ultimate purpose has been achieved, this soul is launched through the roof of the workshop. The body, mind, and persona are like the lower stages of a rocket. As there is ascent, these components are released and burn up with the friction of moving through the atmosphere at impossible speed. It is planned that way. This spectacular equipment will be sacrificed so one small part of the whole apparatus can reach the final destination.

&

Truth is absolutely separate from experience. This is demonstrated by the discrepancy between the amount of proof that different individuals require to live the Truth. How much "proof" does one need? One brief experience of the Truth of unity may be enough for someone to surrender to an awakened life of speech, action, and service. Repeated, daily or almost constant demonstrations through experience of the Reality of nonduality may not be enough for another to submit to living this Truth. The experience means nothing. It's how we use the experience and what kind of willingness and surrender arises as a result of the experience that matters. Our ability to live from the Truth of no-separation unconditionally, regardless of what thoughts, feelings, or sensations arise, is the only thing that matters.

&

Our work is about realizing that it is perfectly appropriate to walk right past thoughts, feelings, and sensations and do nothing more than notice them, not acting on them at all or giving them any fight, but relating to them as remnants and debris of an identity that used to strut its stuff using all of these props to play its part. It is completely appropriate to leave thoughts, feelings, and sensations alone and to use them and express them if and only if they support the expression and transmission of Truth in the moment. Otherwise, they need not be bothered with. When there is absolutely no longer any obligation whatsoever to indulge or engage any arising phenomenon unless it serves the Divine, the Truth, then and only then are we a pure vehicle for Divine will. And this is a simple, simple condition. It is not special. It is full circle all the way back to being an ordinary human being with all the same "inner life," contradictions, and internal manifestations; it is just that the one who is associated with those conditions is now free of bondage to them. Can one be trusted and relied upon to act, speak, and represent what is True and what is in service to union? That is the only question. The arising content of one's inner, psychological, and personal life is completely irrelevant, although its contents could be useful if applied with skillful means, with the right timing, and under the appropriate conditions.

৯

It is most valuable to practice in the face of all kinds of discomforts, especially seemingly small or minor ones. If we don't meditate when we have a cold, or we don't exercise when we're tired, or we pamper ourselves when minor aches and pains arise, we miss the opportunity to map a new relationship between our willingness to practice and discomfort. We have to chip away at the habit of self-coddling when we can so that when the real discomforts arise, as they surely will on the path—psychophysical manifestations of all sorts that will be far stronger than the mere unpleasantries we normally balk at—we stand a chance of staying with our practices and our work. A basic exercise program, for example, is invaluable for this. As, of course, is sitting meditation—and many other practices.

When a commitment toward a specific practice is broken due to a discomfort that unexpectedly arises, either randomly or as a direct result of making the commitment, and at that point one goes back on one's word or commitment, one's practice is not only stalled but is damaged and weakened by not following through. If the commitment is made, one *must* follow through, regardless of the discomfort; otherwise there is no reliable work vehicle for the kind of real sacrifices that must be made for the core Work down the line. Grappling with these petty little commitments and discomforts, if we can handle them successfully, is the surest, if not the only, way to build a practice that can eventually go the distance.

☙

It is a constant and ceaseless struggle to take refuge over and over in God, in the Divine, in no separation, when everything we have trained ourselves to be in response to the separation that is supported by our culture is so powerful and always inviting itself as an option. What does it take for a human being to come to the conclusion that separation is no longer an option? The answer is simple. Only conscious suffering bridges the gap between wanting God and living God. The very pain of separation itself can launch us into a final and impossible-to-prevent dedication to God-life. But this very pain is the pain that we run from, hide from, escape, and deny. Again, why is this? Because our experience as children was that living in no-separation produced so much pain and a perceived threat to our very survival that we had to abandon that Context in order that the animal organism could go on living. To engage spiritual life we have to do an update, look ourselves in the mirror and say, "Hey. I'm not a kid anymore. I can feel pain without falling apart." If we pursue the path long enough, we will eventually discover that real freedom is not avoiding suffering, but rather the certain knowing that there is nothing we can do to stop ourselves from suffering. The idea that we can avoid suffering is actually the only suffering there is.

❧

What the hell, what the hell, what the hell. (Here it comes. An artificially dark rant based on the physiological stress of lack of sleep. But then again, maybe this is exactly when writing could be most valuable, in the moments when one is not strong enough to keep up the veneer.) Where were we? What the hell . . . should one do with all of this? Life, that is. Daily ecstasies and visits to heaven punctuated by moods, thoughts, and actions that are mean, cruel, uncaring, unkind, forgetful, bastardly, and selfish. So what else is new? Well. It's enough to make even the most callous, or green, practitioner think twice about even breathing a wink of anything smacking of "spiritual" experience or realization if one is still capable of being so foul. (And I'm sure one's family would agree).

It's just fucking cruel to hang heaven and hell inside one walking asshole and give him just enough awareness to see it and just enough vulnerability to feel it but not enough integrity to do something about it all.

Ouch.

❧

We all claim to want liberation, to expand into Infinite Love. We imagine that the fact that we do not experience this love and expansiveness is due to superimposed conditions that have been heaped on us and are beyond our control. As if there were a strange and invisible virus floating around that was rendering most of the general public self-centered and mean and it got us too, but maybe someday it will just go away and we'll all be healed up. "Oh, but how I long for God," we pine, while all the time we are actually *actively practicing* limitation and separation. We miss what it is that we ourselves do to prevent our own expansion, because the things we do seem so insignificant, so everyday. But when we add them all up their collective effect is devastating to the Divine, fully truncative of the flow of grace into us. Our thoughts, actions, and speech, like a weak acid doggedly applied, eat away at the foundation of our spiritual efforts, and we are left with nothing but our contractions, our grip on separation. "So what?" we think to ourselves. "I snapped at my wife this morning, no big deal." But if we look at all the moments and see that as the tip of the iceberg, we might find that we were also impatient with the kids at bedtime last night, that we bullied one of our employees or co-workers in the office today a bit, cut off the man who wanted to pull ahead of us into the turn lane, took the last of the main course at dinner when everyone else also wanted more, read our trashy novel instead of cleaning up the house before bed, decided not to send money to the Wildlife Federation this year, glared at the cashier in the store because of the length of the checkout line, told a friend who wanted to talk that we didn't have time, and it goes on from there.

≥

An entity is an independent force living inside a person which uses its host to act on its behalf. Gaining freedom from an entity requires skillful means. We should never try to tear ourselves away from an entity once it has us in its grip. Every entity loves a struggle; in fact, the amount of resistance we put up against it is equal to the entity's strength and vigor. So in the middle of being dragged into the pit of jealousy, rage, greed, desire, whatever it is, we should not resist, but go willingly—and as we are being led by the hand of this beast we should take the energy we would have used to struggle to instead wait and scan for the littlest opening. If the entity does not get the food it desires from the tension of the struggle, its attention will begin to wander, and in the moment that it forgets us for a second, if we are paying attention, we can take the opportunity to escape easily and quickly.

So say we simply must devour a quart of maple-fudge ice cream. Something inside of us is commanding it and we feel helpless in the grip of this desire. If we fight and fight and resist this temptation, we will actually strengthen it to the point that eventually it will gain so much momentum and energy (from our trying to not think about it) that it will finally send us flying into the kitchen, lunging into the freezer, and have us gorging right from the carton with an ice cream scoop before we even know what hit us. So next time this happens, just say to this entity, "Okay, I'll have some ice cream with you." This will shock the hell out of it and set it off balance right from the beginning. As we accompany it to the freezer we should simply pay attention as we get out a bowl, a spoon, and the scoop, but while we are cooperating we should remain open to the possibility that the entity itself could lose interest at any moment. It may not on any particular occasion, but if we have this attitude each time and continue to pay attention, we will begin to find the entity's weak spots and we will see that it does not have, and cannot possess by its very nature, a thing called "intention." Pure intention is unwavering, unforgetful, and specific. Desire is random, cares only to perpetuate the sensation of itself, is fickle, flighty, and prone to loss of its own aim. If we carry attention right next to the entity's desire, we one day will be able to master the art of actually stealing back the energy of that desire. Our attention, held in the right place and in the right way, can cause the energy the entity is using for its temporary and artificial desire to jump tracks and instead feed *our aim*. To accomplish this we must be willing to experiment, be extremely patient and self-forgiving, consider that it's all in the timing of the thing and, again, experiment with that.

And all of this must occur in a mood of yes. As soon as we say no to the whole dynamic, we are dead meat. The whole trick is no resistance. If we can enter whole in relationship to such an entity, we can escape whole. If we resist, we get torn apart from the very beginning and, once fragmented this way, gathering ourselves to make a swift and deft departure from the entity's lair in an opportune moment is impossible.

※

One great sacrifice in a moment of transcendent glory and service to the Divine is nothing compared to an eternity of small, incremental gestures and obedient actions that persist in the face of everything and plod steadily and slowly forward as reliable agents of evolution.

A comet blazing across the sky takes everybody's breath away for an instant, but ultimately affects no one and is soon forgotten. A glacier is rarely ever acknowledged for its movement, which is invisible to the eye, but it changes the face of the earth irrevocably.

It is persistence and consistency that counts. Creating exhaustion due to big or heroic efforts is just another way of avoiding the real practice, the real work, which is the tedium of doing the small, right, appropriate thing time after time, hour after hour, day after day.

The Chinese water torture is designed on the principle of what humans most shun and abhor. Eternity. Eternity kills the mind. Answering each of a child's questions over just a ten-minute period can seem like an eternity. Keeping up with the laundry, responding kindly to the same inelegance from others time and time again, just doing the same dishes in the same way can test our ability to embrace eternity. All forms of impeccability bring us face to face with eternity.

૨❧

Time is the substance that gets created between two presences that are not quite expansive enough to reach each other. The lesser the presence, the greater the appearance of time. Time is an illusion that is created by this lack of presence. It is the phenomenon that arises directly in association with this lack. This substance we call time occupies the void where our presence could be.

When we physically occupy a spot we say that we are "there." When we are not in that spot, we say that the spot is an empty space. Space floods in to fill the physical spot where we are not. In the same way, time streams in to fill the beingness we do not embrace and exude.

When we are being fully, there is no time because there is no room for time there. A fullness of presence exists which does not allow for it.

In a similar vein, when we become aware of Everything as our own body, then we are Everywhere and there is no longer any empty spot; thus, space also disappears.

Time and space only seem to exist to us because we are unable to be present in a way which makes them irrelevant and unable to manifest.

૨❧

Ordinary life is a training and testing period which may result in graduation to the next level of "school" or level of consciousness. Spiritual birth requires full and complete feeling, lack of recoil, and consciousness of the full human experience, including all the attendant sensations, feelings, and nuances of human physical embodiment. If this full feeling is embraced, the second birth process begins, in which consciousness is propelled into an environment which offers a level of stimulus that is profoundly beyond the ordinary, gross level of input available to us through the five sense doors. Once we've "mastered," so to speak, the domain of resting in full feeling in the midst of ordinary life and a "worldly" or fleshy variety of stimuli, we graduate to more refined and challenging forms of energetic food.

In the same way, a fetus is given only a very low level of stimulation, potential for distraction, and sensory input. The conditions in the womb remain somewhat constant and non-volatile—not very complex. This gives the previously unincarnated consciousness a chance to integrate into a new level, that of physical incarnation, without being overwhelmed by the eventual possibilities available to one who has taken physical incarnation. The time spent in utero is a bridge, a sort of decompression chamber where consciousness adjusts itself in stages to a radically altered atmosphere. Once stability is achieved— stability being determined by the ability of consciousness to abide in full awareness at this level of sensory input—birth into the next level of stimulation and input occurs; that is, physical life outside of the mother. This may be why, even today, science still does not know exactly what it is that triggers the actual birth process. It may be that the readiness at the level of the fetus's consciousness is a determining factor.

If a fetus is subjected to a great deal of chemical imbalance, as is the case when it is assaulted by the addictive behavior of a pregnant mother who is abusing alcohol, stimulants, marijuana, or, even more subtly, feelings such as depression, anger, or the presence of constant levels of adrenaline, it is much more difficult for the fetus to stabilize because the consciousness is introduced into an environment which is too complex and volatile for it to build the strength and resiliency it requires to mature naturally into a stable relationship to human embodiment.

Complications arise when, for whatever reason, a premature departure from the safety of the womb becomes necessary for the child. For consciousness to deal with what appears to it as a premature birth is one thing if it occurs under natural circumstances—due to the physical limitations of the mother's ability to carry the child, for instance. In cases, however, when a doctor, or some facet of the established medical system, predetermines the necessity for the birth according to its own timing (e.g., a caesarian is performed so the doctor can make it to tee-off time on schedule—this actually happens), and not according to the timing of the consciousness of the fetus, there is a birth trauma, meaning that the developing consciousness is, to some extent, just a little or perhaps even greatly, unprepared to face the next level of incarnation and its accompanying degree of stimulation and input. So, to one degree or another, we are born into lung-breathing physical life with either perfect readiness, no readiness, or something in between.

The whole model is then applicable to the next stage of incarnation. The care of the mother and father constitutes the external womb from which an infant must slowly and gently ease into its youth with an ability to digest input that is richer, more diverse, complex, challenging to itself as an organism, and even paradoxical to its understanding. If this second womb is not provided, the young child recoils, unable to handle the level of worldly stimulation with which it is confronted, and the child's physical, mental, or emotional growth may become "stunted" at this point by the organism's refusal to move forward without the skills it knows it requires to integrate into the world. The shock of being thrust into too high a level of complexity can be so severe, the survival imperative in the cellular biology of a human being so profound, that in some cases of prolonged neglect to the stage-specific needs of the newborn's development, this stuntedness may not even be correctable or reversible by supplying the proper safety and protection at a later time. Any damage done to the infant's organic and bodily trust, which is the basis of a human being's ability to unfold maturely with respect to interacting with its environment, is repairable only in direct proportion to the degree of shock sustained. At every level of maturity, or birth into a new domain of the evolution of consciousness, the same laws apply.

So, as adults on the spiritual path, our work is to stabilize our own consciousness in a full feeling relationship to all aspects of our present circumstance. This is why before we are allowed to "move on" in spiritual work it is required that we live as a full participant in all the ordinary circumstances of life and are able to do this without recoil or need to turn away from full awareness of any aspect of human reality. This includes thoughts, feelings, sensations, impulses, instincts, desires, and urges.

When this is accomplished, the lawful result of this level of stabilization is the birthing of consciousness into a domain which provides a far greater level of input: psychic, cosmic, and eventually even Infinite. Most human beings, however, as adults, engage in what they believe to be full participation in life without knowing that they are actually distracting themselves from evolving in consciousness. This distraction takes the form of unconsciously creating volatile sensations in the body/mind, the constant bombardment of which overshadows an entire range and host of more subtle and often less "pleasant" sensations and feelings. The distractions take the form of excessively engaging activities such as achievement, recreation and entertainment, physical pleasure, intellectual understanding, control of one's environment and others within one's environment, or the ingestion of chemical substances. The feelings that we are distracting ourselves from are the very same feelings and sensations which arose when we were confronted with circumstances in our early childhood that were too complex for us at the time. Due to the recoil that was associated with these circumstances, the imperative as adults to avoid the remembered terror of being confronted with these feelings too early is profound, and all sorts of distractions are unconsciously sought and perpetuated in order to delay admitting, facing, and integrating them. Integration cannot occur, no matter how "mature" the human organism may be in other areas (e.g., intellectually) until a safe enough environment is created to provide a level of security capable of subsuming the terror that must be faced upon attempting reintegration of these bodily feelings and sensations.

In many cases it is only the profound embodiment of love and compassion that a spiritual master represents which can create a strong enough impression of safety for an individual to gain the faith and strength necessary to participate at this level of reclamation of feeling.

The inability to face or integrate these feelings or sensations into consciousness is felt physically as dis-ease. The more the process of acknowledgment and integration is avoided, the more dis-ease is experienced. The body stores the unembraced feelings and sensations until consciousness is willing and able to allow them to arise out of cellular memory and be processed openly. At some point, the ability for these cells to perform their original and appropriate function can become hampered, or altogether disabled, by their preoccupation with their "guest" (the unprocessed experience). The cell then loses its natural flexibility and rigidifies around what should have been a temporary visitor, and it can no longer perform its rightful duties. At this point it loses integrity—it can no longer participate in the greater body carrying out its natural function—and is now contaminated by the foreign energetic content to the extent that the entire cell is considered to be a foreign agent by the rest of the body and all the other cells in its vicinity. The surrounding cells rigidify in response, the same way the first hosting cell crystallized around the original impurity, and the dis-ease and contamination spread and multiply into the more highly organized systems of the human body. This may be why the phenomenal amount of research that has been dedicated to the treatment of cancer has been, to this date, relatively unsuccessful. Cancer may be the purest and most extremely physicalized form of dis-ease, treatable and preventable only by the strength of the diseased individual's consciousness. There are many other diseases that modern day allopathy treats the symptoms of without ever realizing their real root. The longer one waits to allow such dis-ease to be processed and acknowledged consciously, the more difficult it is to detoxify the cells since there is more and more dis-ease to eliminate or neutralize through awareness as time goes on.

As adults in the Work, our job is two-fold. First, we must stabilize and mature with respect to daily life—ordinary human experience and manifestation at the level of a functional body/mind. Second, we have to build a maturity of practice through which we can continue to function reliably while at the same time we methodically begin to digest the negative impressions which we have stored and held bodily as a result of the premature exposure we received as infants and children to sophisticated levels of emotional, psychic, or physical energy which we were unable to process at the time.

Therapies and growth methodologies that reintroduce such stored traumas without first making sure that the individual is indeed in a position to integrate them in a new way do nothing but reinforce the original traumas. Worse, any kind of spiritual work which involves attempts to trigger higher and infinitely more complex levels of food, stimuli, and experience—especially the energies of unity and the Divine—without first achieving ordinary human stability and a great deal of purification of cellular memory (or karma?) is double trouble and may ultimately produce levels and layers of recoil that are impossible to unravel in the given lifetime of the individual.

It is fundamentally instinct that informs us what degree of input, food, and stimulation is appropriate to any particular level of consciousness. It is solely the introduction of inappropriate expressions of the Divine to human consciousness—that is, manifestations of evolution which are too sophisticated for any particular level of consciousness to swallow—which causes the break, delay, confusion, or corruption of an individual's natural, easeful, and elegant maturation into the embodiment of the disposition of enlightenment. The awareness of this pitfall with respect to human incarnation is crucial to appropriately align our spiritual work to our own level of maturity and our ability to protect and nurture others within the process— especially children, born and unborn.

As we mature in human embodiment, we are able to digest an array of substances—emotional, mental, and even chemical—which at a previous stage of practice would have been detrimental to our development and even permanently poisonous. Just as a yogi might be able to ingest a hallucinogenic drug with seemingly no effect, we become able to participate more and more sophisticatedly with the manifestations of the physical and psychic universe.

All of this is a foundation of understanding on which to base a motive for obedience to the wise elder. Because of the elder's maturity of being and consciousness, he or she can clearly see what forms of input, practice, and circumstances are ultimately appropriate for the student's work. It is only the perfect management of daily activity, life circumstance, food intake (of all types), and skillful use of practice which moves us easefully along the spiritual path. And it is these exact things which the elder offers to determine for us, to guide us in, either directly or indirectly through his influence, and if we are obedient, we can be sure that we will enjoy the most easeful and graceful participation that is possible for us within the great process of Divine evolution.

❧

Some mothers these days harbor the fear that if they give themselves totally to their children they will lose sense of who they are outside of being a mother—frightened that one day, after twenty years of being there for them, they'll wake up after the children are grown and not know who they are. It's a common argument in our "modern" culture, but one which is a product of that culture, not a concern which is integral to being human and a parent. We've been conditioned to believe we must not "put all our eggs in one basket," that we need balance, other interests by which we define ourselves, to avoid this "tragic" situation in which a parent could forget herself, her own "needs." The thing is, if one totally committed oneself to serving his or her children, a loss of identity *could* happen. It puts the possibility and the opportunity of child-raising as a spiritual practice in a powerful light. What modern culture sees as a danger is a great opportunity for a parent who is serious about letting ego wither and shrivel to nothing on the vine.

❧

Long ago we all ran like hell from full feeling in the present moment. Why? Because to live as a child in this culture is like playing football with adults whose bodies have been fully anesthetized, but can still move. Imagine children playing with grown-ups who are numb to their own pain. It doesn't matter how rough the play gets; with skin that doesn't feel, there is nothing to stop them. Nor do they feel the pain when it flashes upward from the bewildered faces of their children, caught on the field of "modern" life, and so they keep on with their busyness, their accomplishments, or in pursuit of their "goals." The children cannot remove their bodies from the insanity of such sport, so they bury their souls in the dirt, hoping one day it will be safe enough to unearth them. This is what God instructs children to do with their souls in such circumstances. But the adults just keep trampling up and down the field. And they are playing to win because, without feeling, that is all there is left to do: win, conquer, defeat the opponent. The capacity to register what it costs those around them was deactivated long ago on the same field at the mercy of adults who they have now become. In this kind of world, numbing out is the only way to be able to stay in the game. And life goes on. The "play" goes on. Things get "done," a lot of television gets watched, and at night, when the curtains are finally drawn, the bodies of all those trapped in such a culture give way to exhaustion. Their muscles, finally relaxing, are unable to muster another task. But the bones of the children never stop aching.

❧

Being neurotic is really no problem—unless, of course, you are a very, or even reasonably, intelligent person, because then you have a means to carry out your very twisted ends. Be neurotic, but be stupid, stumbling, and open about it. Save being intelligent,

131

clever, and sly for when your heart is in the right place. Mixing intelligence and neurosis is deadly to all parties involved. The entire business world is a living demonstration of it.

ᶻᵃ

Any heaviness, lethargy, or pressure we may feel is often only attention itself in a localized and contracted form; what we might call the "cramp." The cramp is nothing more than the localization of a consciousness which is designed to be non-localized and fully expanded. When the energy of our attention is localized, restricted to a small space, as in ego identification, its qualities manifest as solid, dense, thick, heavy, viscous. When we surrender, the same attention is dispersed and expanded to include "all that is," and we experience lightness, peace, bliss, joy, spaciousness, and fluidity.

The process of spiritual evolution runs parallel to the nature of the universe itself. We are in fact a microcosmic demonstration of the truth of the big bang theory. The law of the physics of matter in the universe demands constant movement. The ultimate reflections of this constant movement occur in the extremes of attraction and repulsion, expansion and contraction, that spontaneously and lawfully play themselves out in this eternal flux of matter. The cramp, or ego, is the most dense form of human consciousness. When the contraction of this cramp begins to become conscious in us, it does not release itself immediately. Rather, awareness itself serves to expedite the contraction process and allow the cramp to become fully dense. In this process ego becomes so condensed, implodes so deeply, that it cannot hold itself anymore. At the point at which ego fully saturates itself, reaches maximum density, there is a universal and lawful reflex which acts to disperse the same amount of matter into maximum expansion, and ego "spits itself out." It explodes in what could be equated with the big bang itself—the scattering of that same attention to the ends of Infinity.

This is the entire purpose of self-observation as a practice. Non-judgmental self-observation is not meant to make things better. The very process of self-observation without judgment simply removes the resistance to full contraction and allows for the maximum implosion of ego, which results in the ultimate explosion or expansion of consciousness. That's why things must get much worse before they can get better in this Work. It is all just physics. Once we understand the basic laws and physics of matter and energy at their most fundamental level, we can stop obviating the process. We can cooperate, and things get much quicker and easier, in a way.

&

Why serve? Why be elegant? Why respond to what is wanted and needed? Because the very activity of doing other than this reinforces the illusion of separation. Our unwillingness to serve or recognize Reality does not damage, jeopardize, threaten or lessen that Reality in the least. We do not do these things in support of Reality. Reality needs no support. Our illusion is no threat to Reality. We do our practices only to treat the dis-ease of our own illusion. If we don't, the stream of nonduality still flows merrily along, but if we want to participate in that flow we must become responsible for our interpretation of self. Our view of separate self is reinforced as the perceived reality by the activities of resistance, contrariness, and opposition. A blade of wheat that willfully bends to the west while the rest of the wheat is being naturally windblown to the east creates "proof" or evidence for itself that it is unlike all the others. It may even imagine that it grows in a separate soil or is nourished by a different sun. This, of course, is ridiculous, but not much different from the process by which we, through our own activity, generate appearances that support our story that we are separate.

ॐ

The deepest and most subtle feeling sense in the body *is* the presence of God itself. We come to know this through the body, through being willing to love—that is, feel—the body in its current state and fall into an intimacy with it through the use of our attention. That will take us to a place we never dreamed or imagined we might arrive at through this human vehicle.

We must pay attention. But the degree to which we must pay attention to enter the kingdom of God is not one for which we have a reference. When it is said that we must pay attention, most people think of the level of attention required to keep a car on the road while driving, or to avoid harming ourselves while using a sharp knife. The amount of attention that must be paid is *all* our attention. This comes by completely and totally re-owning, re-assuming, and recollecting all the attention that we normally disburse to various manifestations throughout the universe through the activity of the mind, which is responsible for interpreting, judging, commenting on, assigning meaning to, resisting and desiring more of "what is." If any of this is done to "what is," then we have lost the attention required for entry into God's kingdom. When we cease any activity except the activity of being—that is, being with "what is," feeling every facet and nuance of "what is" with no addition, subtraction, or distortion—what we get in return is the kingdom of God.

This kingdom is a parallel universe that runs perfectly alongside the manifest universe but never intersects the universe of manifestation.

In this universe there is no one and nothing, and it is as obvious, plain, apparent, natural, evident, and rich as the universe of manifestations, but it is never unveiled or revealed until one has absolutely ceased any activity of interpretation of the manifest universe and has entered into an unconditional feeling and present relationship with the manifest universe.

à

When one surrenders, the attention that is liberated—freed from service to the small "s" or separate self—makes it obvious that though all "personal" manifestations continue to arise, there is in fact no one associated with them. There is only that force, that presence, that absence of all qualities, which waits with infinite patience for the drop of water to let itself merge back into the ocean. When bodily relaxation begins to deepen based on the understanding that one cannot do anything for oneself at all—this being proven to oneself through very substantial efforts to do so—there is a natural and effortless journey which begins as one enters a flow of evolutionary power that actually carries one and one's work toward the goal, with nothing required of the practitioner. This, however, only occurs through a profound surrender, and this profound surrender only occurs on a foundation of previous profound efforts.

As the nature of Presence deepens, the Context of what the Divine truly is, is sustained in all activities and in all circumstances as the constant and indestructible undercurrent of all Existence. On the surface nothing has changed, but there is now an understanding, an unwavering undistractibility, that starts to crystallize in the student and makes it ever apparent that the Divine is always active, always present, always the Context in which everything that manifests in the universe arises. To those who have not built a "body" that is capable of perceiving this, these very Divine qualities are invisible and literally impossible to register. The equipment to do so is simply not available.

ॐ

We can't build a practice. Only grace can. We have to earn the intervention of grace by fully engaging our failure to practice. It's all about necessity. With great necessity, we will practice. If we practice—we will fail. With failure, we will be given a living spiritual practice. Not that there will not be failure anymore, but then the failures will be threaded among successes on a necklace of mystery. If we long to wear this mystery more than anything, the failures will be accepted and the successes will not be lauded above the mystery itself.

ॐ

# THE TRUTH OF THE HEART

The cover is taken from the lamp. Its light sears the skin and destroys old eyes. Praise leaps from the heart. You are He, Oh Lord. You are the One that is spoken of. You are the Grace. Caught in the adoration of God knowing Himself through all beings and all things, this small body cannot contain the joy. In rapture and awe it ecstatically hangs on Your sword, lanced by and dangling from the beauty, the ever-presentness, of God's unbelievable and overwhelming affection for All. It has no choice but to leave the realm of confinement to attend the Glory that witnesses God. All is God. You are All.

Oh, Beloved Father. Dropping into Your Arms, weeping like a babe. A heap of tenderness at Your feet. This is like an infectious disease, but please do not let it remit. To pray and serve You is all that remains. Nothing else could possibly repay this debt.

It's all You. It won't stop coming, these waves of energy. With every remembrance and realization that it's all You, the entire body tingles, reels, rises. What an enormous joke! A whole life spent trying to get an aerial view from a submarine; trying to think holy thoughts, act spiritual, have or not have certain feelings. Ha! This wants to be shouted to the whole world. Just be this!

Oh Lord. A hundred years of weeping could not empty the tears from this broken heart, a heart touched by the benediction that You are. Oh, what glory to be nothing, nothing, nothing, and have only "what is" throb and explode in perfect Nothingness and Allness at the same time. You shower Yourself from Everywhere at all times. Let me dare an upturned face to Your Heaven.

෧

Like a newborn waiting for the useless dried up thing called the umbilical cord to fall off, God is waiting for "me" to drop off the belly of Love. This cord, the "I," has served as the conduit for life to enter the real and actual Body, but now it is no longer needed. It is obsolete and rather unsightly. Could this process be FINISHED, please? Let us have it DONE! Such an inappropriate demand. Completely a-lawful. All the same, the heart begs, pleads, grovels for the irrevocable state of disrepair, and prays that this body could live it with no obstruction, break, or delay in its expression.

ेल

It's pure insanity to want God. There is no value in it. It is a disastrous situation for which there is no reward and no gain. It is only ruin. And there is nothing special in it really. No one should want it. Some are simply stricken with this disease of seeking God, which is a totally useless effort and occupation of time and energy, the results of which are not in the least attractive to any individual.

ेल

It all has to return to the realm of the most ordinary, the most regular and unheralded condition. A state of absolutely nothing special, but a condition in which the true Lord, the essence of God Himself, is never forgotten—a condition in which the most exalted bliss of union with the Divine is fused with, married to the most ordinary manifestations of matter in all its forms. In the widest span of consciousness, of voluntary participation in the full and infinite range of existence, such a person dissolves in the infinity of paradox, in the impossible co-existence of opposites, the collision of which leaves not a molecule of universe steady as ground upon which to take up a position.

ॐ

The old habit thinks that stretching ourselves to the breaking point is the thing that will qualify us for love, and that in this way we will earn entry to the Divine kingdom. But if one wants love, then one must stretch oneself to the point of Love, not to the point of breaking. We men have never even considered such a thing before. To stretch to the point of Love is a completely feminine kind of demand, one which most of us have never dared to consider, much less tred the actual path. It is the demand of surrender, as opposed to the other approach, which is masculine: thinking that ego can be beaten into submission, conquered by effort. Love has no walls to scale. It is there, unprotected, undefended, ready for the taking. Since conquest is the relationship the masculine has to everything, approaching Love boggles us. We have to reinvent ourselves in the very first step toward Love.

ॐ

To deeply, deeply let go is a condition in which all that is, is quietly, profoundly, but simply made distinct from anything personal. All the qualities of the embodied individual, all the facets of personality, remain, yet the root identity, the resting place and source of attention, is more and more magnetized by the Lord; by His Grace, Presence, and Influence.

He is the magnificence, the emptiness, and the glory of that which reigns above, beyond, and before any personal life or anything else that was ever conceived. The being must become utterly passive. Then this distinction is clearly delivered by Him.

ॐ

It is astounding, the depth of the ignorance of the "I" that thinks it is going to be able to change things or do any good whatsoever by criticizing, judging, making others wrong, and being right. To drop the habit of feeling that one is obligated to set others straight and to point out their shortcomings is not only the greatest liberation for oneself, but everyone else is even more relieved than we are!

The option to love is always available. Always, always, always. Love is always an option. Love is never inappropriate.

ॐ

During breakfast this morning with the children, Your Glory charmed the mind again. Drinking in the innocence of them brought wonder and amazement. They were so luminous, transparent, so light; angels from another world. As opposed to last night at bedtime when we had a wrestling match in the bathtub, I and my son, while washing his hair. What a scene. Water everywhere, screaming, kicking, splashing, spraying. His father was his greatest enemy for a good twenty minutes, and then, click—he turns it off and is back in arms for stories and sleep, cooing and loving and cuddling. He has no difficulty with such transitions, which is one of the most startling demonstrations of the innocence of children, this acceptance of the moment. This adult mind, however, cannot wrap itself around the diversity of experience that life calls forth. How can life be so transcendent and then so base? So gross and then so subtle? Well, of course, those are just interpretations, but if one is willing to participate bodily, beyond interpretation, in the full spectrum of possible experience, life becomes the cross itself. Horizontal and vertical life colliding in one place called "being human." Then, right there at the heart, there is immeasurable suffering in the effort to reconcile these two realities. In fact, the heart cannot succeed in this.

It only breaks, and eventually surrenders to the impossibility of heaven and hell being spelled out by exactly the same letters: J-U-S-T  T-H-I-S.

❧

It is dancing here now: the Father, so bedazzled, so captivated by and in love with the Mother that everywhere He looks He sees only Her form. And in this captivation He has lost Himself. The Formless Father has completely forgotten Himself—who He is—and has fallen into the Form of the Mother. When Nothing forgets itself, loses itself and surrenders, it becomes Form. When Form's full Attention is stolen by the Beloved, it becomes Formless. This is communion, the true love-making, the lila of the universe, the ultimate sex. It is the lucky person who is aware of the never-ending miracle and utter mystery of this Divine play.

❧

Sometimes fear arises. Will You ever come again? Will the body and heart and mind ever again host Your exquisite charm, be dazzled by the wonder of Your unmapped Form, your unseen torrent of Grace? Sometimes it seems as though You will not come again, but in the midst of this despair You give the gift of Remembrance and the knowledge that it is only this concern itself that can render separation from You. Then a little patience returns to the body. On its heels a song of faith stirs in the heart, and before long the soul hears Your symphony again.

Oh, Beloved, please let it get worse—much worse. Bring on the full disaster, the tameless hurricane of Your blessing. Like an unhappy piñata, dangling like loneliness on a string, this heart is longing to be hit hard enough to be scattered on the floor, strewn about in pieces, devoured by Your happy children.

❦

The man of the heart is a man with no address. His residence is the heart of every other. He, in fact, has no heart himself, but finds himself only in the abandonment of his own emotion, thought, or attitude. The man of the heart gives up everything in the hopelessness of ever finding love; the moment he gives up the search, the heart finds him and never leaves him unless he begins to search for it again.

There are two possible lives: the life of search and the life of surrender. The searcher is like one who bangs pots together while hunting for wild game. The quarry, of course, flees. The surrenderer is the one who has the deer eating out of his hand by remaining still, broken, and devoid of ambition. Wild game can sense a trophy hunter from miles away.

❦

What a spectacular game and grand lila. "Do you want me or do you want Me?" is the question God is always posing, the test that is always being offered. "Because if you want me with a small 'm'," He says, "then you can have me in a million different ways. I am endless, boundless, limitless, and I will exhaust you and eat you up and use you to feed my grand machine. But if you want Me with a capital 'M', you must ignore, and look through, all of me with the small 'm'. Every last manifestation, every nuance, every object, everything. If you look only to Me as creator of all the rest, then it is I that shall feed you, and you shall sit by my side and live while the rest of the world perishes in the satisfaction of its little hungers. I am the highest desire. The desire of desire. So desire away, but let your desire become an unquenchable and insatiable desire. Such a desire that only One, and One alone, can quench your thirst. Want Me with all your heart and soul and marrow. You may use 'me' to get the fire started whenever you need, but as the fire roars, remember Me as the only flame of desire which is pure and everlasting."

❧

Beloved. You are breaking this heart. Here in its cave, it knows nothing. You are too immense and cannot be kept inside. No one could accept the burden of this adoration except You Yourself. But when the heart turns to You to discharge what is burning within, opening to release it, what happens? You come streaming in! And then it is more unbearable. Better stop, slow down, take a break, the body counsels. But You do not cease. You flood and gush into the veins. Until now this lover was only proud. Feeling special. Now he just hurts. But do not imagine that this breaking man is wandering around with an agony about his face. This intimacy will not be announced except to share it by Your command. The blood boils in private.

❧

You make it clear, Beloved, that each of these experiences—these raptures—is just another straw on the camel's back. So be it. Let there be work and more work to add straw after straw until the

**145**

camel collapses. But this work will not be drudgery, or hard time done in a labor camp, no. This work will be endless joy because this work is nothing more than not taking one's eye from You. This work is the supreme and endless enjoyment of Your billion forms in every instant and moment of life. Everywhere and at every turn the heart sees only You, and declares Your glory.

è

This whole life has been a searching. Searching and seeking for You. But there is no one seeking You anymore. The seeking is no longer. It has turned to reveling in You. Marveling and wondering, breathing You, walking in You. The birds fly by in You. The air swirls skyward because of You. So now what? What now, Oh Lord? There is only one thing. To fall more and more deeply into Your bottomless pit of Just This. Just You. It is a strange life, a strange existence, to be living as many characters, but having these repeated visits and glimpses from the One.

è

Tonight, though quietly going to bed in this world, there is no leave of You. No one knows, not even the heart itself, what this is, what You are. The profoundly certain, quiet, unspoken and longing joy that is just there, pulsing beneath the activity of the day. You, Oh Lord, are the day itself, and when it is done, as now, this body rests in the Infinity that will tomorrow breathe the body out into You once more. By the world of appearances there seems to be a dance, a coming and going, but You are the Infinity as well, and so, in Truth, there is nothing happening. No day. No night. Just You.

ॐ

Words cannot ever say it, but they tempt and tease and give more rope to hang oneself with in longing. Words can come close, very close, but it is like this: The words seem to promise that if one will only jump one will reach the other side through expression, truly communicating something. Instead, the possibility of uttering one True word or sentence only entices one to jump, but the other side is never reached. Only the silence grows in return, and one more broken poet becomes food for Your Abyss.

ॐ

It could not be any simpler. Everyone should know. Any effort one can make toward spiritual practice on earth—all seeking and trying and learning—is just a warmup, preparation to be able to do one thing and one thing only: to put oneself in the hands of a saint; to be able to give our attention to a Teacher who has chosen to accept our confused and restless state into His company and let this attention grow and grow. It is very, very simple, but so few make this their reality. The more one's attention is absorbed by the Teacher, the less attention there is for this thing called "one-self." And when attention stops going to the little self, that self is diminished, shrinks from lack of feeding. The more this shift of attention is surrendered to, the more any sense of a separate individual self or "I" disappears. It is this simple. Turn to Him. There is no other. If Everywhere and always one is with Him and sees Him, there will be no room in the mind for one to exist. If there is no room in the mind, there is no room in Reality. If any-thing other than Him is important, it is impossible to know Every-thing. Knowing Every-thing is the natural state of awareness that is present when any-thing ceases to be important anymore. Because the Teacher is not limited, not a thing, putting one's attention there is the only safe haven, the only shelter in which the mind can take refuge without getting wet. All other refuges are faulty, with many holes in the roof, most without roofs altogether.

※

The mind is a collection of ideas, a stream of thoughts that have been herded together so long they believe they need each other to survive. Like a sheep dog that runs around wildly, even over the backs of the beasts to keep them together, the mind is no more than a sheep herder. Its fundamental task is to turn a large number of sheep into one manageable and controllable entity. Just as the flock is an artificial grouping of essentially free animals, the "I" is an artificial herd of ideas and beliefs that are free and distinct, belonging to no one. Let them go now, and let God's presence reign supreme in this little space that has been defended as "me" for so long.

※

The perfect release of all but exactly This shall be the dedication of this life, just to please You, just to honor You, as a demonstration of gratitude laid at Your feet. There is nothing left. And when the mind is found seeking, the Remembrance of You, here and now, will bring the heart back to Your throne. To desire anything else in the face of each moment which is You is ignorance itself, is the only suffering, the only possible bondage. To realize You—the completeness, perfection, and glory of You—as this very moment, this very body, this very life, is the whole work. Let there be nothing but worship left in this life. Each instant is a temple where You sit on the center of the altar in Your splendor, there for any to enjoy if they will but lift their eyes.

è‰

This expansion, the glory of this devastation, is indescribable and useless. There is nothing that can be done with it, no place on this planet in which it can be traded, sold, recognized, or understood.

Who would want it? No one understands. Especially those who become it. It is, in fact, impossible to understand, and trying to understand is the only thing that separates us from the knowledge that we are nothing but You.

è‰

When "helping" others in the past, especially in groups, this "leader" used to really get off on dismantling their status quo, on challenging them, shaking them up, taking their position apart with logic, group energy, manipulation of emotion, and use of cathartic techniques. What ignorance. Only You, only Grace can dissolve the status quo. Like the way light handles darkness. It doesn't destroy what used to be there, it just comes in, and what used to occupy the space prior to its coming is simply and promptly forgotten.

è‰

Everything must be given back to Him again and again. Only complete surrender can provide a safe haven for the Universe to pass right through us. It is all Him. The peace and bliss of resting in all as Him. No resistance, just an empty channel through which "what is" passes and is seen only as Him. What joy this is, to be an instrument of His music.

Being utterly surrendered is the pinnacle of spirituality.

≈

God is resident in every particle of the Universe. When this is unveiled, unmasked, every particle radiates the immeasurable Love of God and shouts through its mask, through its disguise, that it is only God Himself, only a form to be reveled in and enjoyed as God. This is Grace, the act of God manifesting Himself in form, and when that form is known in its Truth, seen in its Truth, the Grace of God explodes in the being of the beholder and the beholder is overcome, suffused with, and blown apart by the immensity of God's compassion and Grace. The luminosity is almost unbearable, completely consuming.

≈

You, Beloved, are the only life and breath. Here and Now, in the footsteps of Your Grace, Oh Lord, are the skeletons of acknowledgment and status, of reward and even hope. Does all this babble make a difference? Does it come absolutely and purely from the heart? YES! Only You. Only You. The body quivers, aches, is destroyed and rises again in You. Because of You. Is this madness? Complete and utter delusion? Maybe.

The body goes on. Life goes on. Perhaps no one will ever know. But You will know. And You may claim all of this at any time, at any moment. It is rightfully Yours. Where can this go from here? What is this that is being said? Surely these are only the bold gushings of imagination and fantasy. But it is so imagined that it has become Real enough to drench the heart with tears that are full of Love for You. Ah . . . so easy it is to touch this here in an empty room, late at night, all alone. What about the rest of the day and the rest of the world? Let the full force of this Love beat Everywhere, all the time, without cease and without end. Oh Beloved! This cannot be declared to anyone but You. The rest of the world will see an alien, a poor, mind-broken, deluded, brainwashed sucker who has lost all sanity. How much stronger would this devotion have to become, how much deeper would it have to reach, to permanently destroy the harmful one? How much more must be shattered for him to become truly benign? Swallowed whole by You, the beast is not yet fully digested. It awaits the moment when it becomes only food to feed Your Great Body, nutrition for Your limbs. May there be only the thought of You.

&#2360;

At the full effect of Your brutal Reality the body bends, buckles, thrills. Out of the blue You creep up, invisibly, silently. You get bigger and bigger, more and more present, and this is when You become known as Presence. The spine then madly tingles, hairs bristle with a kind of terror that is as seductive as it is frightening. As You loom more and more present in that moment, consuming absolutely Everything, all at once what used to be only objects are transformed into You as Presence, and the body cannot contain, hold, or exist in the immensity of You. The pure energy that floods in accumulates in the spine, limbs, and joints at a massive rate and must be unloaded. So the body cracks. It jumps, jolts, falls down, flings its arms violently into the air, or cries out in unknown voices.

Now the body is tired. It lobbies for a slowdown, to take a break. The heart does not want a break. It wants to be broken. But the heart is not independent of the body, and this is the reason for all practice: to train, discipline, and purify the body so it is able to accompany the heart into the blinding chamber of Your Love.

🙚

A question arose and You answered it, saying that the aim of this path is to be in a constant state of prayer and functional at the same time. When You said that word, "prayer," it was like a gong being struck that is still sounding on. Even in the midst of experiences of unity it hadn't occurred to this one that holding those experiences as prayer—in the distinct and singular mood of prayer—would be the key to sustaining and integrating them into the rest of life; to being in a state of prayer all the time.

🙚

You are a secret omnipresence that most never see. There is so much sleep in these eyes, but when they are awake to You, You are so obvious, naturally Present in Everything, *as* Everything. Brimming with joy, delight, gratitude, and awe, every moment of Your appearance is profound wonder to this one. At first You would snatch away the veil in random instants of surprise. Then Your perfume would waft upon the scene a few moments before Your Infinite Body arrived, and there was a sense of You just about to pop out of the woodwork. Now that perfume lingers when You have gone, dallying round the heart, and even when You are gone there is the feeling that You are right there, as possibility—that the possibility of Your unveiling is permanently true, permanently present. You are either present as Presence, or as the possibility of that Presence, in every moment.

As attention falls into You as Presence, it is as if the glue which has always bound the molecules of this body/mind together gets dissolved. Then the "I" stretches and expands at a violent rate, explosively scattering this tangle of dilemma to Everything and Everywhere all at once. What is left is "what is." And "what is" is so sublime, so chartless, so supreme, so simple, delightful, and liberating that the heart is stunned by it, made drunk by it. The mind ceases in its tracks and the grip it has on any-thing automatically releases, lets go . . .

Let this prayer be repeated incessantly for the Gods to hear. May there be nothing but this. Nothing but this. Nothing but this!

❧

There is nothing to do but to serve You. From day to day and moment to moment there is nothing but the shadowy and unverifiable stirrings of instinct for guidance, which I follow with as much obedience as can be mustered, hoping and praying that it makes some difference to You. There is nothing else. Nothing. So let there be patience, trust, and more work until it is clear that the right things are being attended to, if that ever happens. After all, it is just ego that feels as though it is not serving unless it has a big task, a magnificent and earth-shattering project or responsibility.

At least there is faith. It is not any accomplishment, it is only a response to the trustworthiness of You. You are all that is needed, the only One needed to remember, rely on, open to, give full attention to. You are Faith.

ે

Your breath is hot upon the neck. You will devour this charade completely in one instant. When that instant will be is unknowable, but still the moment is felt—so near, so looming. You are going to snap the neck of this mind swift and clean and forever. Tell me, who is the one who is longing for this?

ે

What do You want? How long do You want this limbo to go on? Here underneath the intense pressure of Your Divine thumb, this bug begs you to do it a favor and lean a little harder, just enough to squash it and have it done. Ha! How deluded is this? Maybe light years, or perhaps lifetimes, lie between this and actually awakening into radical service to You. We're just entering preparatory stages and the body is already complaining about a little pressure—a little discomfort. But this is all new territory; a little ignorance (or a lot) can be expected, can it not? Please tolerate Your self-absorbed disciple. Who knows? Maybe it will be beneficial to pretend that something Real is close. What does it matter if the right sacrifices get made out of ignorance and delusion? There should be such luck. The mind is relentless, the body resistant, but the heart is already packing to leave this halfway house. It wants to come Home.

ે

Every morning in meditation there is a deep drop into God's being, a fresh wash, bathed in the glory of God's perfection. But then the day's responsibilities are allowed to gradually eat away at the precious jewel of Remembrance. How serious can the practice of such a person be? It is true that to live an ordinary life in the world and feed one's connection to God simultaneously is a challenging path. But excuses do not satisfy the heart that wants to be lost in this rapture, wants to swoon and fall into God all the time. Nothing else is going to successfully disintegrate what it is that needs to be taken apart. The glue that binds this cloud of "self"-concern called "me" is long hardened and resilient. It will need to soak for quite some time to be dissolved, to unveil the fog and show the baselessness of all the personal pettiness which prevails.

When things are going well and "I" start to feel good about "my" work, the guard goes down, and before long, wham, there "I" am again making the same old mistakes. Feeling like one is progressing or working well just supports the contraction of one as an individual, doing something.

❧

We are literally just walking portable antennae, designed to be able to channel God, the Divine, from heaven, from Everywhere, to the earth, and to shine out that heaven to all who live and breathe here. Our attention is meant to be on God so that we can use this body, which is made for a dual purpose, as a bridge—to take the revelatory energy of God's Grace and put it into action here so that it may be demonstrated, felt, and known by as many as possible. The design is for man to be a middleman—just a distributor of God's product. Let us be Your middleman, Oh Lord. Make this our aim. Make this our destiny. Use us! Make us a clear channel for Your

Influence, Your Love. Make us pure, make us harmless, take our personal wishes and aims.

&

Now what? "Now what?" is the question. Truly, truly stumped—in bliss, in delight and the ecstasy of God—the mind has been stopped dead in its tracks. Shall there be sleep? Or shall this madness be declared to a world of deafness? Is it better to wait for God's irrefutable direction, or to let such madness have its way? Shall the children be simply loved until they walk one day into lives of their own? What shall be done?

Who is kidding whom? There is still seeking here. It is lurking still, waiting, looking for something more. And so the mind seeks what it calls "the final undoing." But how shall that be found when the seeker makes such laughable efforts? Who is still seeking? What an impossible mess this is. The finished and the unfinished living in the same room, breathing the same air. Which will it be? Which is it? Come and resolve this chaos if You will, Lord. Or is this chaos the way it will always be now? How do You like these silly questions?

Please finish this dangling man, this creature with his head half off, hanging over the abyss. Give him the full void. Sharpen up the guillotine and let it be a clean blow; permanent severance is required. The body/mind itself? Who cares? Let it claw its way through the rest of its days, panicked and self-possessed. That's all it can do anyway. Let it run. What damage can it do? It is well enough socialized and trained to keep the peace.

But set the soul free. Now please. There is no going back for this one. Set it fully free. Only You can do this, God.

❧

When the mind has been overtaken by His Grace, there is great joy, but at other times it is worried, restless and grasping, wondering whether or not it will again be blessed with His Presence. But the heart cannot imagine a life not steeped in God: His Blessing, His burning and ever-present monopolization of its attention. There is nothing else it wants except to be consumed by Him. The heart wants to be taken over, annihilated, made no more, scattered out on the wind of prayer. But God, the Lord, is the Master, and He comes and goes as He pleases, and the heart is left to beg His Grace, His silent and invisible gaze. The heart longs for this, lives only for this.

❧

Only You. Everything and Nothing. All is being made perfectly nothing under the annihilating force of Your Gaze, being made utterly empty, utterly full—complete. The cells of the physical and spiritual body are ripped apart, scattered to Infinity, and reorganized under Your Name. Everything is known through Your Name, consumed by the rhythm of Your Heart. Destroyed by nothing but Your presence, all is blinded by Your resplendent Grace to Everything but You Everywhere.

❧

This morning in meditation, once again, came the feeling of teetering on the brink of extinction. And how will this extinction occur? From the sheer size and immensity of You, Beloved Lord! The mind, heart, body, and soul unravel in . . . what? Divine terror—the most delicious terror ever known. Brought to its knees, each cell in the body is bathed in the awe of God's Infinity. The breath halts, is taken away, then labors, as though breathing a new substance, completely unknown—so thick, so vast, so dense, so charged that the body is thrown into complete and rapt wonder. And . . . it is not big enough yet. Still, all the old habits remain! God takes the heart to His sweet endless Paradise, then commands the body to open its eyes, stand up, and go about the day. So it does. Living just on the edge of God, feeling God, still seeing God Everywhere, though pretending to be normal, the body is just waiting. Waiting for God to bring it completely and permanently Home.

❧

Only God is important. What else could anyone want? The bliss of gazing inwardly at His beautiful, beautiful Face, His Eyes, His Form. Total distraction in God can only happen through His Grace. And His Grace is the fact of existence here on planet earth; accessible, available. There is no other possibility. This is the Blessing of God.

❧

Everything everywhere—every thought, feeling, sensation, object, concept, happening, experience, movement, and change—is God. There is no possibility of anything else. It is all One thing. Yet the final realization of this Truth eludes the mind completely and courts only the heart. Only surrender, complete and utter, will do. It cannot be done alone. Patience, trust, and faith are demanded more than ever. This one is slowly melting in Grace and Love. God is taking every last old joy, every tired comfort, every possible alternative piece by piece, cell by cell, moment by moment.

₰

The whole body is on alert, tingling with longing, aching to be devoured by what is True. Like some eager prey who feels the hunter lurking in a silent shadow, the breath is sweet with terror, all senses completely heightened. The heart pounds in anticipation of the One who will take all and give Nothing in return. This is the enchanted forest where the prey prays and the Hunter does not hunt, but only waits until the game has sped itself upon His arrow.

₰

Thank you for these words. To be purified by the boldness of them and brought up by them, challenged by them, is a blessing. Let this life bow in obedience to the purity of the Teaching. This is the only option. Let there be work and work and more work until this is the case. Until all people who come across this life only feel that they have come across what is obedient to the Truth. This is the heart's only wish.

₰

Oh Lord! The floodgates have opened. Tears gush from this heart, split open by Your Grace, the sweetest tears ever wrung from this lost, lost, utterly lost soul come home to You. The heart is broken! It beholds all as itself. Who could believe such Glory? Oh, Beloved. My love! Can it be so?

It is only the effort itself of wanting to be something, wanting to be special, that has allowed this defeat by You. It is the intensity of the effort alone that allowed for complete failure and ripened the heart to resort only to You. Only You. Without all the effort, You may not have won. But the effort showed the futility of the search, the weakness of the searcher, and the impossibility of self-delivery. You stood aside while the inner war raged, and once all defenses were completely occupied with the wrong opponent, You stepped into the ring and won with a kiss. Now, I am down for the count, weeping with gratitude. You are Lord of another surrendered and broken heart.

All victory to You, Oh God. May You win them All! May every heart be undone by You, made nothing, broken in love. This brokenness is ONLY HUMAN! It is not special, extraordinary, or any pinnacle of achievement. It is only the natural condition of being human, of being alive. This suffering, this brokenness, hurts so fine. It hurts so fine. With pain this sweet, who would not consent to be human forever? This is just the way it should be for a human being. It is the natural condition of being human, the true nature of humanness. So raw and so new. It is like being a new babe, but this babe, instead of wanting his mother, just wants his Father.

෨෧

Now the woman is here, waiting to be entered. Trusting more and more deeply. Waiting for her Beloved. She can do nothing but wait and long and imagine and Love, gazing at the Beloved and knowing that she is His—has always been His. He will take her in His time, and she will wait Forever if that is what it takes. There is only His Love.

෨෧

Ah, so this is the root of beggarship. When one is praying that his bowl will remain empty until God comes to fill it. When the world comes into his bowl, he eats what is offered right away so the body might be perpetuated for another hour of longing, or he throws it into the gutter if it cannot sustain his longing. Only the empty bowl can receive Him, entice Him. The empty bowl is the demonstration of hunger which the beggar of God uses to plead for mercy. Empty, empty, empty all the time. Only God is good enough for the true beggar's bowl.

꤯

# ADDITIONAL TITLES FROM HOHM PRESS

*THE ALCHEMY OF TRANSFORMATION*
by Lee Lozowick
Foreword by Claudio Naranjo, M.D.

"I really appreciate Lee's message. The world needs to hear his God-talk. It's insightful and healing."—John White, author, and editor, *What is Enlightenment?: Exploring the Goal of the Spiritual Path.*

A concise and straightforward overview of the principles of spiritual life as developed and taught by Lee Lozowick for the past twenty years in the West. Subjects of use to seekers and serious students of any spiritual tradition include: • From self-centeredness to God-centeredness • The role of a Teacher and a practice in spiritual life • The job of the community in "self"-liberation • Longing and devotion. Lee Lozowick's spiritual tradition is that of the western Baul, related in teaching and spirit to the Bauls of Bengal, India. *The Alchemy of Transformation* presents his radical, elegant and irreverent approach to human alchemical transformation.

Paper, 192 pages, $14.95                    ISBN: 0-934252-62-9

• • •

*AS IT IS: A Year on the Road with a Tantric Teacher*
by M. Young

A first-hand account of a one-year journey around the world in the company of a *tantric* teacher. This book catalogues the trials and wonders of day-to-day interactions between a teacher and his students, and presents a broad range of his teachings given in seminars from San Francisco, California to Rishikesh, India. *As It Is* considers the core principles of *tantra*, including non-duality, compassion (the Bodhisattva ideal), service to others and transformation within daily life. Written as a narrative, this captivating book will appeal to practitioners of *any* spiritual path. Readers interested in a life of clarity, genuine creativity, wisdom and harmony will find this an invaluable resource.

Paper, 840 pages, 24 b&w photos, $29.95          ISBN: 0-934252-99-8

# ADDITIONAL TITLES FROM HOHM PRESS

*HALFWAY UP THE MOUNTAIN*
*The Error of Premature Claims to Enlightenment*
by Mariana Caplan                                    Foreword by Fleet Maull

Dozens of first-hand interviews with students, respected spiritual teachers and masters, together with broad research are synthesized here to assist readers in avoiding the pitfalls of the spiritual path. Topics include: mistaking mystical experience for enlightenment; ego inflation, power and corruption among spiritual leaders; the question of the need for a teacher; disillusionment on the path...and much more.

"Caplan's illuminating book...urges seekers to pay the price of traveling the hard road to true enlightenment." —*Publisher's Weekly*

Paper, 600 pages, $21.95                                    ISBN: 0-934252-91-2

• • •

*THE SHADOW ON THE PATH*
*Clearing the Psychological Blocks to Spiritual Development*
by VJ Fedorschak                                    Foreword by Claudio Naranjo, M.D.

Tracing the development of the human psychological shadow from Freud to the present, this readable analysis presents five contemporary approaches to spiritual psychotherapy for those who find themselves needing help on the spiritual path. Offers insight into the phenomenon of denial and projection.

Topics include: the shadow in the work of notable therapists; the principles of inner spiritual development in the major world religions; examples of the disowned shadow in contemporary religious movements; and case studies of clients in spiritual groups who have worked with their shadow issues.

Paper, 324 pages, $17.95                                    ISBN: 0-934252-81-5

• • •

*SIT: Zen Teachings of Master Taisen Deshimaru*
edited by Philippe Coupey

"To understand oneself is to understand the universe." – *Master Taisen Deshimaru*

Like spending a month in retreat with a great Zen master, *SIT* addresses the practice of meditation for both beginners and long-time students of Zen. Deshimaru's powerful and insightful approach is particularly suited to those who desire an experience of the rigorous Soto tradition in a form that is accessible to Westerners.

Paper, 375 pages, $19.95                                    ISBN: 0-934252-61-0

**TO ORDER PLEASE SEE ACCOMPANYING ORDER FORM
OR CALL 1-800-381-2700 TO PLACE YOUR ORDER NOW.
VISIT OUR WEBSITE: www.hohmpress.com**

# ADDITIONAL TITLES FROM HOHM PRESS

## THE ONLY GRACE IS LOVING GOD
by Lee Lozowick

Love, God, Loving God, Grace, Divine Will—these subjects have engaged the minds and hearts of theologians throughout the ages, and even caused radical schisms within organized religions. Lee Lozowick dares to address them again, and in a way entirely original. He challenges all conventional definitions of love, and all superficial assumptions about the nature of loving God, and introduces a radical distinction which he calls the "whim of God" to explain why the random and beneficent Grace of loving God is humanity's ultimate possibility. More than just esoteric musings, *The Only Grace is Loving God* is an urgent and practical appeal to every hungry heart.

Paper, 108 pages, $5.95                                                ISBN: 0-934252-07-6

• • •

## THE YOGA TRADITION: *Its History, Literature, Philosophy and Practice*
by Georg Feuerstein, Ph.D.                                   Foreword by Ken Wilber

A complete overview of the great Yogic traditions of: Raja-Yoga, Hatha-Yoga, Jnana-Yoga, Bhakti-Yoga, Karma-Yoga, Tantra-Yoga, Kundalini-Yoga, Mantra-Yoga and many other lesser known forms. Includes translations of over twenty famous Yoga treatises, like the *Yoga-Sutra* of Patanjali, and a first-time translation of the *Goraksha Paddhati*, an ancient Hatha Yoga text. Covers all aspects of Hindu, Buddhist, Jaina and Sikh Yoga. A necessary resource for all students and scholars of Yoga.

"Without a doubt the finest overall explanation of Yoga. Destined to become a classic." – Ken Wilber

Paper, 708 pages, Over 200 illustrations, $39.95          ISBN: 0-934252-83-1
Cloth, $49.95                                                             ISBN: 0-934252-88-2

• • •

## RUMI — THIEF OF SLEEP
*180 Quatrains from the Persian*
Translations by Shahram Shiva; Foreword by Deepak Chopra

This book contains 180 translations of Rumi's short devotional poems, or *quatrains*. Shiva's versions are based on his own carefully documented translation from the Farsi (Persian), the language in which Rumi wrote.

"In *Thief of Sleep*, Shahram Shiva (who embodies the culture, the wisdom and the history of Sufism in his very genes) brings us the healing experience. I recommend his book to anyone who wishes *to remember.* This book will help you do that." —Deepak Chopra, author of *How to Know God.*

Paper, 120 pages, $11.95                                            ISBN: 1-890772-05-4

**TO ORDER PLEASE SEE ACCOMPANYING ORDER FORM OR CALL 1-800-381-2700 TO PLACE YOUR ORDER NOW. VISIT OUR WEBSITE: www.hohmpress.com**

# RETAIL ORDER FORM FOR HOHM PRESS BOOKS

Name_____ Phone ( ) _____

Street Address or P.O. Box _____

City _____ State _____ Zip Code _____

| QTY | TITLE | ITEM PRICE | TOTAL PRICE |
|-----|-------|-----------|-------------|
| | THE ALCHEMY OF TRANSFORMATION | $14.95 | |
| | AS IT IS | $29.95 | |
| | HALFWAY UP THE MOUNTAIN | $21.95 | |
| | THE ONLY GRACE IS LOVING GOD | $5.95 | |
| | THE PERFECTION OF NOTHING | $14.95 | |
| | RUMI-THIEF OF SLEEP | $11.95 | |
| | THE SHADOW ON THE PATH | $17.95 | |
| | SIT | $19.95 | |
| | YOGA TRADITION - PAPER | $39.95 | |
| | YOGA TRADITION - CLOTH | $49.95 | |

**SURFACE SHIPPING CHARGES**

1st book ................................................ $5.00

Each additional item ............................. $1.00

SUBTOTAL: ___

SHIPPING: (see below) ___

TOTAL: ___

**SHIP MY ORDER**

☐ Surface U.S. Mail—Priority     ☐ UPS (Mail + $2.00)

☐ 2nd-Day Air (Mail + $5.00)     ☐ Next-Day Air (Mail + $15.00)

**METHOD OF PAYMENT:**

☐ Check or M.O.    Payable to Hohm Press, P.O. Box 2501, Prescott, AZ 86302

☐ Call 1-800-381-2700 to place your credit card order

☐ Or call 1-520-717-1779 to fax your credit card order

☐ Information for Visa/MasterCard/American Express order only:

Card #_____ –_____ –_____ –_____

Expiration Date_____

*Visit our Website to view our complete catalog: www.hohmpress.com*

*ORDER NOW!*

*Call 1-800-381-2700 or fax your order to 1-520-717-1779.*

*(Remember to include your credit card information.)*